ADVANCE PRAISE

"In *Un-Settling*, Maggie McReynolds gives voice to what needs to be validated for newly divorced women who likely suffer in silence. She has written from the wisdom of her own experience and shared her soul in this refreshing, vulnerable account. Along with useful strategies and life-changing wisdom, this book is the best support and a grounding read for anyone who has ever doubted and struggled with their decision to divorce and cope with life after divorce.

I'm honored to completely recommend this book to my patients, friends, and anyone who has experienced divorce."

Dr. Denise Morett
Licensed Psychologist and best-selling author of *LIFELINE: A Parent's Guide to Coping with a Child's Serious or Life-Threatening Medical Issue.*

₃childwithmedicalissues.com/

T0163659

I found *Un-Settling* a breath of fresh air. As a child of a "good" divorce in the 70s (my parents co-parented, easily attended functions together—my mom and stepmom even road tripped together to visit my sister and me at college)—I still know how easy it can be for a divorced mom to doubt her decisions and worry about her children's well-being. Maggie McReynolds has clearly experienced the pain, angst and guilt of a divorcing parent but her own experiences as well as that of her clients weaves a narrative that uplifts and empowers anyone who is walking down that path. We often are told to let go of our past but more importantly, *Un-Settling* guides the reader to create and step into the best life she can imagine. And in the end, perhaps that is the most amazing gift we can give our children after all."

Gina Catalano
Coach and author of *Tandem Leadership:*
How Your #2 Can Make You #1

"*Un-Settling* is a must-read for any divorced mom worrying about her kids. By weaving together stories of her past, her present life, and the successes of her clients, Maggie draws the reader in and paints a compelling picture of how the *Un-Settling* process helps divorced moms and their kids find meaningful happiness and abundance. As she points out, we aren't born to settle—but settling can and often does set in post-divorce. Maggie's guidance and exercises are perfect for the mom who wants to model what living a full, *Un-Settling* life looks like for her children. An entertaining and informative read, with easy-to-understand action steps and a game-changing take on life after divorce."

Cassie Parks
Money Manifestation Expert
www.manifest10k.com/

"What a wonderful book for those who are divorcing and unwilling to settle for a less-than life. With sections such as "Creating a New Us" and "The Art of Self-Forgiveness," this book reads like a good friend telling you how she not only how she got through her divorce, but how she got through it *well*. Bravo!"

Robin Rice

Social Change Artist and author of
A Hundred Ways to Sunday
www.robinrice.com/

"Breakups are never fun, and even less so when children are involved. Maggie McReynolds removes a lot of the agony by sharing the stories of how she and her clients have navigated marital change with hope, courage and a big dose of positive self-talk. This book is a must have for moms at any point in the separation and divorce process.

Mara Linaberger

Author of *HELP! My Child Hates School:
An Awakened Parent's Guide to Action*
www.maralinaberger.com

Un-Settling

Un-Settling

How *to*
Help Your Kids *by*
Making *and* Modeling
an AMAZING Life
After Divorce

Maggie McReynolds

NEW YORK

LONDON • NASHVILLE • MELBOURNE • VANCOUVER

Un-Settling

How to Help Your Kids by Making and Modeling an Amazing Life After Divorce

Published in New York, New York, by Morgan James Publishing in partnership with Difference Press. Morgan James is a trademark of Morgan James, LLC. www.MorganJamesPublishing.com

The Morgan James Speakers Group can bring authors to your live event. For more information or to book an event visit The Morgan James Speakers Group at www.TheMorganJamesSpeakersGroup.com.

ISBN 9781683507413 paperback
ISBN 9781683507420 eBook
Library of Congress Control Number: 2017913310

Cover Design by:
Rachel Lopez
www.r2cdesign.com

Interior Design by:
Chris Treccani
www.3dogcreative.net

In an effort to support local communities, raise awareness and funds, Morgan James Publishing donates a percentage of all book sales for the life of each book to Habitat for Humanity Peninsula and Greater Williamsburg.

Get involved today! Visit
www.MorganJamesBuilds.com

For my mom, an *Un-Settling Woman* who was smart enough to cut her losses and brave enough to kick free

TABLE OF CONTENTS

INTRODUCTION

*It had been almost three months since the divorce was final,
and once again she was awake and restless in the small hours
of the morning.*

*She dragged her laptop onto the bed. She Googled "age kids
disconnect" and found neither comfort nor consensus. She
Googled "single mom work-life balance" and realized she'd
already clicked through the first 45 links that came up. She
Googled "how long after divorce until life feels normal,"
afraid to even look at the answer.*

*She Googled charter schools, day spas, therapists, and
summer camps. Finally, after a long space of time in which
she realized she was just zoning out and staring dully at the
screen, she moved the cursor to the search bar and slowly
typed, "Help."*

*The Beatles didn't have the answer to the real question that
was keeping her up at night:*

How could she make sure her kids were going to be okay?

Not so long ago, this was basically me. My ex and I had chosen to end our marriage because we were both spent, exhausted by trying to hold still and settle for a pale echo of what we'd once had. The tipping point, for us, was the realization of what we were modeling for our son: that this was what marriage was, sleeping in separate rooms, arguing late at night, avoiding each other during the day. We both wanted better, not just for ourselves, but also for him.

That belief in some undefined "better" sustained me as I leapt into the unknown. But even though I had both the hope and intention of building a happy new normal for me and my son, I was unprepared for my anxiety levels shooting off the charts. In that first year, I worried almost constantly about whether my son was struggling at school, if he was making friends, and about whether he'd be able to form lasting, positive relationships, let alone get married himself. Was he crying himself to sleep, or, worse, waking up and crying, alone, in the middle of the night? Was the divorce an emotional wound that would scar him for life?

I can't tell you how many divorced moms I've worked with who tell me this is pretty much exactly what swirls through their heads when they can't sleep. We are worry machines, stuck in the "on" position. Google is our go-to, our late-night frenemy. It never seems to have quite the answers we seek—but that doesn't stop us from trying, night after restless night.

I staved off some of the initial anxiety after my ex moved out by staying in near-constant motion. I redecorated the master bedroom, gutted the master bath, repainted my son's bedroom, and directed a crew of subcontractors to fix all the things my handy but overworked and distractible ex-husband had always meant to get around to fixing, but didn't. You probably did some of this, too. Do you remember the first thing you bought that you knew your ex would have hated? (I found it weirdly exhilarating.)

But once my renovation budget and my enthusiasm for comparing paint chips ran out, there I was with the rest of my life—our life—yawning before me. And I realized I didn't know what to do with it. The calls were now all mine to make, which was sort of exciting, but I felt hobbled by my anxiety over my son's emotional equilibrium. I measured everything against whether it would make up for the way I perceived his dad and I had let him down. All the choices seemed too big; the potential consequences too huge. And so we hung in limbo, a post-divorce purgatory. Why couldn't I find the clarity and confidence I'd brought to my decision to end my marriage now that I was a divorced, single mom?

Whatever clear-eyed, decisive mojo I'd found, it seemed like I'd misplaced it. You too?

I'd been clear and confident by nature at one time—back when my ex and I met as juniors in college. I'd wanted him and acted on it; we moved in together after only three months of dating. We were motivated in part by economics (why keep two apartments when we were really only using one?), but mostly by how beautifully we matched. We were both writers, worshiped movies, had amazing conversations, and were good at making each other and others laugh. We went on to start a company together, write together, and do virtually everything together.

We didn't even spend our first night apart until five years later, after we were married.

Then I got sick. After almost a year of baffling and increasingly severe symptoms that masqueraded as everything from rheumatoid arthritis to multiple sclerosis, I was diagnosed with Chronic Fatigue Syndrome at age 29. We were still college sweethearts emotionally, and my sudden-onset illness sort of froze us there. While other couples were maturing and starting families and making five-year plans, we were learning to settle for sheer survival, just trying to get from one day to the next.

It was bad. My ex, who had a genetic tendency toward depression, sought therapy to cope and was misdiagnosed with bipolar disorder. I was so sick I had to go back to bed after my morning shower and rest on the landing before I could make it all the way up the stairs. He struggled more or less alone on an increasingly dizzying cocktail of medications he didn't need that were only making things worse. I cried and clamored and complained; he shut down, went cold, and withdrew. We both confessed years later, once we had each recovered and stabilized, that we would have left during this period if we'd thought the other strong enough to survive alone.

We loved each other; we muddled through. But when our son was born ten years later, it became clear that while we knew how to be companionate kids together (us against the world!), illness had prevented us from learning how to be cooperative adults in charge of a new human being. We adored our new boy, but we couldn't seem to get into a routine. We became baton parents, handing the baby back and forth so the other could work (one of our son's first full sentences was, "Take him!"). We slept in different rooms (I was co-sleeping; my ex had insomnia); we kept to different schedules. We didn't watch movies, or play music, or even hang out together anymore. As we slowly came apart, it became easier to nurse grudges and harbor unresolved resentment. The fissures left over from our early years of health crises became bigger cracks, then chasms.

We tried therapy, but we came to it too late, after we'd sort of given up. We were exhausted and unable to find a way forward; there certainly wasn't any way to go back. I think we were both surprised to find that love did not, in the end, prove to be enough. We agreed, as amicably as you can when your heart is broken, to divorce.

Your divorce experience is, of course, your own. And whatever took you from "as long as we both shall live" to "I want out" was uniquely painful. But we all have this in common: none of us go into marriage expecting it to end. None of us are really prepared for what happens after it does.

Even when we know for sure that we want a divorce, we can't know in advance what it will be like to actually *be* divorced and parenting on our own. And it's hard, isn't it? Harder than you thought it would be. You hoped for a second chance at happiness, and for your kids to be happy, too. How come changing what feels like everything didn't make everything better?

Worry is normal. It's what we moms do. But in the emotional aftermath of divorce and all the second-guessing over whether we did *the right thing for the kids*, that worry can disconnect us from our inner warrior mom, the one who was determined to stop settling, willing to make hard choices, and resolute in modeling something better for her kids.

We lose touch with the very woman our kids most need us to be in order to know that everything is going to be okay.

Remember when your kids began taking their first steps and inevitably fell on their diapered behinds? They looked to you, didn't they? They watched your face for their cue as to how they should respond. If you seemed upset, or cried out, or rushed over to them, they figured something terrible had happened and they wailed, hurt or not. If you were matter-of-fact and communicated that the fall was unfortunate, but recoverable, they probably got right back up and tried to walk again.

They looked to you then for how to move forward; they are looking to you still. Even though divorce is considerably more complicated and its effects more far-reaching than recovery from a simple fall-down-go-boom, you have the same choice before you: model fear and the belief that the world is an unsafe and unsatisfying place; or model confidence and the willingness to take good risks in order to create an amazing life.

Can it be that the very thing you fear will cause your kids lifelong pain—all the turmoil that comes with divorce—might also be their saving grace? Could the refusal to settle that led you to end your marriage be the very gift you're meant to pass down?

If you're struggling to believe that, know that I didn't start out there, either. I was sure that if I worried hard enough and long enough, if I suffered a little, even, that I could make up for my son's pain over something he didn't sign up for. I worried, I suffered, I got sick, I got sicker—and none of it helped my son, not even a little bit. That's when I realized I needed to come at life after divorce differently, and that's ultimately why I wrote this book. I want to share with you all that I wish someone had told me, back when I was beating myself up and second-guessing my every move.

I found my power—and my son's happiness—not in settling for a small, fretful, anxiety-filled life after divorce, but in *Un-Settling*: remembering the woman I'd grown to be and knowing in my soul that this refusal to settle for less-than would serve me and my son more than one more moment spent in anxiety or despair. *Un-Settling* was a game-changer; it knit new bonds between us and created more possibility than I had ever imagined. *Un-Settling* saved us, and it became the core of what I teach the divorced moms I coach.

Un-Settling is more than a single decision, though it starts with one. It's a way of being, one we'll explore together in the following pages. We'll take a look at who you are as a newly divorced mom and why you're a great parent even when it doesn't feel like it. We'll talk about how to create joy and abundance for you and your kids, and learn the secrets of some of the smartest, most successful, single moms I know. You'll figure out how to build the foundation for a great new relationship with your kids and even an effective co-parenting relationship with your ex, no matter what led to your divorce. We'll make sure your kids are better than okay.

Nobody goes into marriage *or* parenthood believing they're going to get divorced. But by choosing to stop settling, you open yourself up to the infinite possibilities of *Un-Settling*, and you take on the rest of your life and your kids' lives in a powerful way. Divorce is an ending, but it's also a beginning. Take heart, remember who you are and all that you're capable of, and hold onto hope. Things are about to get a whole lot better.

CHAPTER ONE

Plot Twist

"I want a divorce," she'd said. And just like that, life as she'd
known it was over.
It had been just about the hardest thing she'd ever done, but she
hadn't let that stop her. She'd grabbed her kids' hands and jumped.
She knew there was something better out there for all of them.
So it was good news/bad news. They hadn't crashed and burned,
but neither had they yet triumphantly soared. She had hoped for
some clear sign, some unequivocal success to prove that she hadn't
been completely selfish and that she hadn't messed up her kids
beyond repair. Instead, her kids were alternatively distant and
crabby and the cat had started peeing on a corner of the rug.
She heard raised voices, coming from the direction of the kitchen.
Why did all the fights seem to happen in front of an open
refrigerator door?

My client Daria thought she had been married to a great guy. As it turned out, there were a few other women who thought so, too. By the time Daria got the full measure of her ex-husband's infidelities, he had slept his way, she told me, through what seemed like a third of the PTA. Daria didn't just feel betrayed, she also felt deeply humiliated. The whole school seemed to know what had taken her a couple of years to figure out.

She didn't want to go back—she wasn't going to settle for marriage to a liar and a philanderer—but neither was she clear on how to find her way forward. I met Daria about three months after her divorce was final, and about a year after she'd left the family home. "I moved out," she told me, "because I just couldn't stand being in that house, in that neighborhood, taking the kids to school and seeing all those moms who *knew*."

Daria and the kids had moved into a modest condo closer to downtown. It was nice enough, she told me, but life felt small and muted. The kids had wanted to move—they were old enough to know what was going on, and they were embarrassed, too—but they were trying to make their way in a new school, and it seemed like they spent a lot of time in their new, tinier, bedrooms. She worried that they resented her even more than they resented their dad. And even though she understood that her prior happiness had been based on illusion, she missed both the expansiveness of her former life—they had lived in a lovely, oversize Colonial in one of the area's more prestigious suburbs—as well as having a concrete vision of the future. "We had it all mapped out," she said. "Where we'd move after the kids graduated from high school, where we'd travel, where we'd retire. I don't know what I want now. I don't know how to make my kids happy. I don't know if I can travel or when I can retire on my own."

Daria had done plenty of grieving over the loss of the life she'd thought she was going to lead, and had worked with a therapist to get through the worst of it. But now that she had more or less let it all go, she felt unmoored. Without a clear vision of her new life, releasing the past had felt like sailing away from the only shore she'd ever known with no other destination in sight. The horizon was beautiful and seemed like it could hold promise. But it was also scary and surprisingly lonely.

Like me, like Daria, you chose to divorce your husband, maybe on your own initiative, maybe in response to an untenable situation, provocation, or circumstance. But having made that choice can feel like both blessing and curse. There's true empowerment in having finally seized the reins of your life and taken action. There may also be gut-churning angst, sporadic fits of guilt, and more than a little second-guessing over what you chose.

No matter how clear you may be on your decision—you wouldn't go back—you may not yet see a clear way forward like you expected. Isn't it supposed to be easier than this? Instead of feeling your way into your new normal, you're anxious, exhausted, overwhelmed, and watching your kids like a hawk for signs of emotional turbulence and damage. You left because you didn't want to settle for the life you'd been living. But the life you exchanged it for is beginning to feel a little like settling for a different kind of hard.

The post-divorce world can initially seem like a blizzard of opportunity—you can do anything! But it's also a little like Single Mom Prison, and your fear shapes the bars. You can't move your kids out of state unless your ex says it's okay. And there are school districts and friendships and not-rocking-the-boat-more-than-you-already-have conundrums. With only one income now, you feel that you have to make careful choices about what to spend your money on. Ugh, you probably need more life insurance.

Your kids aren't a burden. You adore being a mom. But your single parenthood is a huge factor in every decision you'll make going forward. Your kids' emotional well-being—are they really okay, and how can you be sure?—is at the top of your list. Your responsibilities—to be your household's sole breadwinner, to somehow make it all up to your kids, to keep all the trains running on time—don't exactly feel conducive to problem-solving and self-exploration, let alone transformational adventure. You don't even know who you are now, as a parent or a person. You love the idea of building the happy, balanced, new normal you thought awaited you on the other side of your divorce. You want to make everything okay for your kids. But you have no idea where to even start.

This is the point at which I meet most of my clients, that liminal space between their old lives and the still embryonic new ones. The adrenaline surge that comes with taking big and brave action has faded, and acute grief has begun to be replaced by chronic anxiety. What if you screw up your kids even more than the divorce probably already has? What if you let the fear of doing so paralyze you into living a small, desperate life?

No wonder we get stuck! With so much seemingly at risk, we hunker down because it doesn't feel safe to stand tall. It took so much energy—*so much energy*—just to make that final call, get out, and get through the legalities of ending a marriage. How do we muster the will, the courage, and the vision to move the ball forward from here without incurring more damage? How do we create a new life in which there's one fewer setting at the table, one less toothbrush in the holder, without our kids falling into the hole our divorce created for them? We stopped settling for a marriage that was less-than. How do we stop settling for a less-than life after divorce?

Some of us, like my client Sophie, hope that holding still will translate into our kids' feeling safe and secure. Sophie fought hard to keep the family home. She didn't want to move her son away from his friends and out of his school district. And after all she'd been through, she told me, she deserved to have that house. She was proud of keeping everything as much the same as she could for her boy.

Some things, however, were out of her control. Her son seemed … kind of okay. But he had started biting his nails again and bringing once-forbidden junk food into the family room while he watched TV, a practice she'd discouraged before the divorce. He was looking as pudgy as she sometimes felt.

And then there were her neighborhood friends. She thought everybody would rally around, and some did. Others talked a lot about how they'd be in touch, but then drifted away. A couple of them treated her like she was suddenly going to go after their husbands, which was insulting as well as the furthest thing from her mind. She wasn't sure she wanted to date again, ever. She certainly didn't want to get involved with one of her friends' husbands. She'd been listening to their wives complain about them for years.

Sometimes, she told me, she felt like she was living in a museum, a shrine to the life she used to lead. There were echoes of her marriage everywhere, from the family pictures she'd left out for her son's sake to the marital bed she still slept in. Her son was on dog poop duty instead of her ex, and she now took out the garbage, but other than the empty side of the closet where suits used to hang, things didn't feel all that different from when her ex was away on a business trip. She'd even continued Meatball Mondays—she didn't like meatballs—because her son had cried the first time she'd suggested changing things up.

Sophie had struggled to figure out who she was and what she wanted back in college. Now she was trying to figure out the same things while juggling a career, single parenting, and some semblance of a social life. The potential consequences of making a wrong move and "screwing things up even more" for her and for her son weighed heavily on her. She'd already shaken things up enough, she felt, by getting a divorce. What if she made another leap and found she was suddenly Wile E. Coyote, plummeting off a cliff and desperately trying to cobble together some kind of soft landing with ACME tools and duct tape on her way down?

Both of these women had defined their new lives either by change or by the lack of it. On the one hand there was Daria, who had moved, not entirely happily, and who had a lot of fear that even if she could come up with a "what's-next" wish list, she wouldn't be able to fulfill it. Like more than a few of my divorced clients, she joked, with a little too much edge, about becoming a "crazy cat lady." She wanted to be close to her kids; she worried that they were withdrawing, and didn't know how to stop the drift. Even though she had primary custody, she often felt isolated, and she was afraid her relationship with her kids had taken a permanent hit from which it would never recover.

On the other hand, there was Sophie, who had changed things up as little as humanly possible and was second-guessing whether that had been the right choice. Maybe she and her son would be in a better place if she'd given them a fresh start. Maybe if she'd thrown out the pictures, or moved, or, hey, even changed Meatball Mondays to, say, Manicotti Mondays, she'd feel less stuck. Almost a year later, and she still kept expecting her ex to pull into the driveway (which of course he still did, but now only Tuesday nights and every other Friday when it was his turn to have their son).

Daria and Sophie didn't see the ways in which they were still settling until I took each of them through the process of figuring out who they were post-divorce and then redefining and expanding upon their goals for themselves and their kids. Daria came to see that she had been settling for a smaller life than she'd led before because she was afraid she wasn't "enough" as a single parent to claim bigger dreams; Sophie realized she'd been settling for the deceptive safety of familiarity because she was afraid her son couldn't cope with yet another transition. They had lost the momentum and impact of the clear, decisive energy they had brought to their divorces, and post-divorce anxiety had become their driving force. But with fresh awareness of the ways in which they'd been unconsciously contributing to their own pain and keeping themselves small, both women were able to reclaim their second chances at happiness and take steps toward creating it for themselves and their kids. They remembered themselves and what they were capable of, and were able to act from their power as *Un-Settling Women*.

Both women had looked outside themselves to define their lives post-divorce. I get it; I did that, too. After my ex left, I was determined to stay in the family home, and then, a year later, I was equally determined to leave it. I can see now that while this wasn't meaningless—it was the only house my son had known—it wasn't the make-or-break choice I thought it was back then. What was important was my relationship with myself and my relationship with my kid, not the setting in which those relationships took place. I am both proud and embarrassed to say that it took my own kid pointing this out to me for me to get it. "I don't care where we live, Mom," he said, "as long as we're happy."

External change is right in front of our faces and at the forefront of our consciousness, so of course it seems like changing things out there is what will change things inside. And yet, focusing on externals without leading from within is just a different kind of settling. When we shift our perspective slightly, we can see that we've got it backward. It's when *we* change—even if we change something as seemingly insignificant as a single thought—that everything out there begins to shift. What needs to happen starts to come into focus. The next steps appear, surprisingly obvious and gratifyingly doable. We move past paralysis and into clarity of vision. We begin to get on with our lives. *Un-Settling* becomes our come-from, our credo, our model for how to have the life we always dreamed of. Our kids follow our lead, and learn how to build amazing lives of their own.

This is good news—the best news, really. We have control here, and we can do something. The change we want to see in the world, in our lives, and in our children, begins with us.

Divorce is awful. But its aftermath is one of the richest opportunities you'll ever be given to redefine yourself, dream big dreams, and make bold, life-defining choices about who you are, how you want to parent, what you want to model for your kids, and what kind of experience and impact you want to have in the world. Divorce is the beginning of *Un-Settling*, and of claiming the absolute best of the only life you'll ever lead as this particular human, in this space of time.

It sounds big, but the next steps are small, and in the following pages, we'll walk through each of them. As you read on, know this: you already have everything you need to create and model the life you want for you and your kids.

CHAPTER TWO

How to Know If You're Settling

She'd forgotten to take the change-of-address form to the school office. Again.

She frowned and scrolled through her other emails, trying to ignore the noise emanating from somewhere behind her head. What were the neighbors doing over there? It sounded like they had chained the furniture and were busy dragging it around. She wasn't used to having a shared wall.

"My head is going to explode," she thought.

Flipping over to Facebook, she clicked on a lentil recipe that sounded quick and promising. Right, like anybody would eat it but her. Dinners had devolved into pizza, pizza, Chinese, guilt chicken, and pizza.

She'd always done most of the cooking and cleaning, but ever since the divorce, she felt like either she never had time to shop or she was too tired to cook.

"Mom?" called a voice from down the hall. "What's for dinner?"
She thumbed her phone for the number for Shanghai Sue's while
the neighbors heaved what sounded like an anvil across the room.
In her mind, her head vaporized in a cloud of dust.

We end our marriages and hope we did the right thing, even as we worry that we have messed our kids up in some way that may not even reveal itself until adulthood. As a child of divorce myself, I was *so determined* not to do the same thing to my kid—and yet I did. Sometimes making the tough call is the right thing to do. The willingness to do so is, after all, part of our job description.

I know that despite my fear of history repeating itself, having gone through it before was of benefit, too. I was lucky to have been raised by an *Un-Settling Mother*. If she could be brave under far more challenging circumstances, so could I.

My mom had been thinking of leaving my dad almost since the honeymoon, but what clinched it for her was the day he began rolling around on the floor during one of their arguments, punching himself in the stomach and screaming that he was a terrible husband and father.

Horrifyingly, he'd done this sort of thing before. One time, he'd careened the family car around the highway and threatened to kill us all by driving into an abutment. Dad was tormented by a unique kind of self-loathing; he claimed to believe that he struggled under the watchful eye of two different gods, Goot and Terris, whose sole purpose was to make his life distinctly and profoundly bad. He was bright, funny, and wildly imaginative, and when he was not threatening to kill himself or us, he could be truly a magical, engaged, and entertaining father. He was also mentally ill and strongly disinclined to get help.

What was different about that particular day was that for the first time during one of these episodes, I was awake, in the room, and just barely old enough, at age two, to know something was terribly wrong. Frightened, I cried and ran to him, begging him to tell me what was hurting and how I could help. That, my mom has always told me, was that. She had been willing to "settle" for the weird roller coaster ride her marriage had become when it was only her well-being on the line—for better or for worse, right? But she was not willing to settle for that for me.

Would it help you to know that I am grateful they divorced? Once my dad didn't have my mother around to act as either buffer or punching bag (yes, he hit her, too), he turned out to be a surprisingly good father, albeit an eccentric one, and I continued to have a mostly positive relationship with him. But I didn't have to live with the day-to-day crazy, and that was paramount. I'm proud of my mom for making such a hard but necessary choice, especially back when divorce wasn't as common as it is today, and when she had no college education or career to fall back on.

She moved me downstate, found us a place to live, and took on a series of low-paying jobs—all she could find—to support us. When she needed medical care and couldn't afford the lab work-up, she talked the doctor into finding her a job at the hospital simply by showing him her budget. She started as a lab tech, got a two-year degree as an operating room technician, and then worked full-time while also going to school full-time to become an RN. It doesn't surprise me that she ended up as a psych nurse. We had both learned to be wary of and fascinated by mental illness from dealing with my dad.

All along the way, my mother refused to settle. When I cried every day at daycare, she somehow found the money for my magical nanny Mary Jane, who shared my passions for *Mighty Mouse* and hot tea loaded with milk and sugar. Although Mom attracted plenty of men (she was only 26 and looked something like Julie Andrews), she passed up dozens who had little interest in and affinity for parenting a toddler in favor of the one guy she met—the man who would become my stepfather—who loved me just as much as she did. Every Christmas was spectacular, no matter the state of our family finances, with magic and ritual and mountains of presents, including one special one for each of us wrapped in an elaborate glitter painting she'd done entirely by hand. By the time my sister was eight and I was 13, we were regularly traveling to Wyoming to backpack and camp the mountain passes in Grand Teton National Park. I cherish a picture of my mom, one eye closed against the shampoo, shrieking and washing her hair in an ice-cold, spring-fed mountain stream, because she refused to go one more day "with this awful, greasy hair!"

My mom lives in Arizona now, with the walk-in bathtub from her wish list and the swimming pool she always dreamed of in her backyard. But every time she travels somewhere, she settles in with Craigslist or the local want ads. Not because she isn't happy with where she is, but because you never know when the next adventure will present itself, and she wants to be ready.

I learned how to be an *Un-Settling Mother*—and an *Un-Settling Woman*—from my mom, and that served me well when my ex and I chose to split. I was able to take a crummy situation and hold fast to the belief that I could find and mine the gold in it. Her courage helped me move cross-country, seek out a team of specialists and go from bedridden to highly functional, become a life coach, get my son into an academically challenging charter school, support his music, find love, and claim a much larger life than the one that had presented itself, post-divorce, to me. I'm grateful for her modeling independence and the refusal to settle. I see now that her actions didn't predispose me to divorce, as I had feared; instead, they gave me the perspective I needed to make the best choices possible for me and my son.

Born to *Un-Settle*

We were all *Un-Settling*, once. You probably don't remember much from back when you were two or three, but you almost certainly remember your kids at that age. No, they said. NO! they bellowed. No, no, no, no, *no,* they repeated until you wished they'd never learned the word in the first place. They had discovered the power of choice and the thrill of not just agitating for what they wanted, but also of refusing to accept what they didn't.

We, as a society, do our best to train this right out of them.

When we are very young, we are natural *Un-Settlers*. We are pirates, sailing the ship of our beds windward. We are space explorers, blasting off to the moon in a cardboard box. We are fluid, certain that girls can grow up to be men, and boys, women, and that either gender can transform into any animal of our choosing. At one point, I believed quite fervently that I was a cat named Musette.

But then we go to school. And as we settle into our seats and behind our desks, we enter into the Academy of Settling. In the name of being socialized, in the name of being *fair*, we are herded, homogenized, and taught that our particular spark is, if not unimportant, then certainly not entirely welcome. Raise your hand. Form a line. Wait your turn. Here's what you can do, but here's an even bigger list of all the things that you can't. We are taught that it's wrong to inconvenience others by standing out, taking risks, getting ahead of the group. All of us are supposed to arrive at the same place, and at the same time.

Did you watch this happen to your kids? Do you remember it happening to you?

Through deeply embedded and almost imperceptible practices of punishment, isolation, and shaming, we become the young adults, the people, and even the parents that we've been unknowingly training all our lives to be. We *settle* into the patterns laid out for us. It's easy, as easy as a wagon wheel settling into a rut worn by every traveler who came before. Settling into that rut feels natural, and trying to get ourselves out of it seems harsh, disruptive, bumpy, and dangerous. What if a wheel comes right off? What even worse experience will we have to settle for, then?

Some of us go through a bit of a teen rebellion. For others of us, choosing to end our marriage can be the first significant act of *Un-Settling* we've undertaken since childhood. We've been dutiful. We've done the right thing. We've played by the rules of college-marriage-house-kids. Things have to get pretty uncomfortable before we are willing to jump our wheel out of the rut and take a chance on something better. It goes against everything we were taught to do.

This single brave move, this bold and perhaps unaccustomed act of *Un-Settling*, can be thrilling—and it can exhaust us to the point of paralysis and frighten us into a return to playing small. We are worry machines, remember? And we're so worried about our kids! But this can also be our pivot point, if we let it. We can seize our decision and leverage its momentum into a new life of *Un-Settling* choices. We can model something better than what we grew up with or ended up, at one point, settling for.

My client Jess, who had been married three times, had settled into a pattern of alternating rage and depression by the time she came to work with me. Jess was not only stuck processing her last marriage, she had yet to work through her feelings from her first. Jumping from one relationship to the next is a fiendishly effective strategy for not having to deal with your stuff—and it also means your stuff grows exponentially with each failed pairing. By the time I worked with Jess, she had stockpiled a couple decades' worth of resentment and she was giving herself the experience that being in a marriage— any marriage, really—was superior to living helplessly with the anger that would surface in between brief bouts of marital bliss. Her daughter had learned to tune out and get by as best she could—she'd taken to wearing earbuds all the time, even when they weren't plugged into anything. They were both settling for pain of the known (the rut) over the risk of the unfamiliar.

None of us perpetuate terrible situations without getting something that serves us out of them. I'll just duck here while you take a swing at me, but after, if you think about it, you'll realize the inherent truth in this. I stayed in my marriage, for example, in part because I was giving myself a rich opportunity to work through any lingering feelings of abandonment by my father (my mom may have done the leaving, but my dad had abandoned us, even involuntarily, for mental illness long before). Jess, as it turned out, needed her anger desperately. It was a placeholder emotion for deep sadness and low self-esteem, and it felt like something close to power. Infinitely better, Jess had unconsciously reasoned, than succumbing to despair.

Jess and I worked together to identify who she was without a man at her side (she'd never given herself much time to know) and where she wanted to be, which she was able to identify as independent, self-supporting, in touch with her feelings, and in touch with her similarly angry teenage daughter. A poet and a gifted sculptor, Jess was a natural *Un-Settler*, and the first step on her path was literally as simple as making one single decision. (I'll tell you what it was a little later on.)

She no longer believes divorce is worse than any of her marriages. In fact, she's successfully raised a brilliant young woman and is busy making plans to retire overseas. Her exuberant artwork graces my home.

In a relatively short space of time, Jess mastered the art of *Un-Settling:* manifesting the life she wanted to live, leading with intention, holding strong boundaries that brought ease to her relationship with her kid, and finding her best path toward the abundance that made her new life with her daughter possible.

In the rest of this book, we'll talk about how you can do this, too.

Settling for Fear

We don't always see the ways in which we are still settling for less-than after divorce, because those ways are sneaky and masquerade as doing "the right thing." But settling has a "tell," just like a card shark faking you out with a bluff. Settling is driven primarily by fear. When we operate from fear, we are settling for the rut. It's a narrow and uncomfortable path, isn't it?

After divorce, you can assume fear is in the driver's seat when you find yourself giving in to one of what I call The Three S Words:

- **Shame**—You swore you'd never get divorced, and yet here you are. You still can't believe you let yourself and your kids down. You are a terrible mom.
- **Second-guessing**—Maybe it wasn't so bad. Maybe you shouldn't have left. Maybe an "intact" family, no matter how dysfunctional, is better than a "broken" one. You are not enough.
- **Stress**—You don't sleep well. Your diet is even worse. You are running as fast as you can, but it feels like you're on a hamster wheel and you never get to a destination you haven't even identified yet. You want to puke.

Hello, fear! In each of the above lurks the worry that keeps you tossing and turning at night: you made a mistake, you messed up your kids, you messed up the rest of your life, you'll end up eating cat food filched from a dumpster, you'll die alone or maybe find a partner but make the same mistakes all over again, which will mean, eventually, dying alone anyway. Oh, and your kids will wind up in broken marriages just like you, which you may or may not know about because they may never speak to you again.

Settling like a Good Girl

When we are in grade school, aka the Academy of Settling, conforming and compliance are rewarded. You are told you are a "good girl." And so we dutifully draw flowers when we'd rather draw dragons, sit quietly in chairs even though we absorb information better when we are in motion, share toys we're not ready to let go of, and play four square at recess even though we'd rather shoot hoops with the boys or read by ourselves under a tree. This is not all bad—we learn to be kind, generous, and considerate—but neither is it all good. We also learn to hide or sublimate our needs and wants because yearning for something different—or, heaven forbid, better—is considered greedy, unseemly, and ungrateful.

We are indoctrinated in the fine art of sighing and settling, of accepting the status quo without looking too closely at the set of limitations it really is. Sure, we may have had a teenage rebellion; perhaps we even colored outside the lines a bit here and there. But mostly, we followed the rules—until the unthinkable happened: we divorced. We've been "bad," by Academy of Settling standards. We've boldly and publicly declared our want for something different, something better, and we've shaken up our kids' lives to try and get it.

For many women, the cognitive dissonance generated by "I made the best choice I could for my kids" alongside "I destroyed life as they knew it" is a fierce, white-hot pain. The natural response is to want to move away from the flame. Where's a bad girl to go in order to feel better about herself and her choices? You guessed it: right back to being a good girl—or, at this point in your life, a Good Mom.

This can look like almost anything, but might show up as:

- Staying in a house you don't like, can't afford, or have no good memories of so that your kids have continuity
- Stretching beyond your means to continue extracurricular activities so your kids won't feel like they've lost everything
- Deferring goals of your own in favor of trying to "make it up" to the kids
- Sacrificing a social life in the belief your kids need you at their side every moment they're home
- Letting boundaries blur and house rules slide because the kids are hurting and you want them to be happy
- Spending time you don't have volunteering at the school because you want to keep an eye on your kids
- Going without regular hair, dental, doctor, and other appointments for self-care either to spend the money on your kids or because you don't "deserve" it

The twisted reward for this kind of settling is that no one will look at you and judge your choices. From the outside, you look like a dedicated and devoted mom. But you ended your marriage because you wanted to model something better for your kids. What is martyrdom and self-sacrifice teaching them, and are you sure that's the lesson you want to put across?

The *Un-Settling* Truth

Are you settling? Are you living smaller than you and your kids deserve? Are you allowing fear to hold you back from making and modeling the life you want for you and you children?

If you're reading this book, the answer is most likely yes—just like pretty much every other divorced mom out there. It's a natural consequence of taking an action that appears to contradict every Good Mom rule you've been taught or even invented for yourself. But where are you settling, and by how much? Just like getting a handle on your spending helps you find your way out of debt, getting a handle on where and how you are settling helps you find your way to *Un-Settling* and creating the kind of life you want your kids to learn from and, one day, lead.

We can't do better until we know better. That means that identifying the thoughts, behaviors, and beliefs that stand in your way is key in order to take those first steps to free yourself and your kids from the pain you've all been experiencing post-divorce. Like Daria and Sophie, you are most likely unaware of all the ways in which you are settling, and teaching your kids to settle, too. I know you don't want that; none of us do. So stop settling right here: take this short quiz, The Un-Settling Truth, and let's get clear on what's working, and what's a roadblock we can learn to kick aside or go around. Your results will be relevant as we move forward through the *Un-Settling* process in the rest of this book.

CHAPTER THREE

What's Your Story?

When each of her children were born, she felt compelled to tell the story of her labor and their birth, over and over. A doula told her at the time that it was an important part of processing the emotions of the experience.

Now she found herself recounting the story of her divorce to anyone who would listen, including herself. She replayed how it had gone down in her head, questioning his choices, her choices, everything that had led up to the devastating decision they had ultimately come to. She felt like she was caught in a time loop; she worried that she was starting to bore her friends. She had gone on one single date since the divorce, and she was embarrassed and horrified that she had spent most of their dinner talking about her ex.

What was going on? Why couldn't she just shut up and let it go?

S tories are how we process and communicate the things that happen to us. But they can also be what keep us settled and toeing the line. Our parents and the adults at the Academy of Settling encourage us to be autonomous—but not *too* autonomous. By example and by spoken cliché, we learn the rules and the clearly marked limits. We learn that we can't trust ourselves or our peers. ("If your friend told you to jump off a cliff, would you do that, too?") We learn that wanting things is wrong and that abundance is hard to acquire. ("Money doesn't grow on trees, you know!") We learn to shut up and accept the status quo. ("If you don't have anything nice to say, don't say anything at all!")

Our books and our movies advocate settling, too. Cinderella is a passive victim of circumstance who sings about her big dreams while slavishly scrubbing floors; her only way out is to be rescued by a fairy godmother, magical mice, and a Prince. Little Red Riding Hood shows some gumption by trying to find medicine for her sick grandmother, but because she takes "the wrong path" (no metaphors here, nope!), she almost gets eaten by a wolf. Dorothy learns that she was wrong to yearn for adventure because "there's no place like home."

The stories we were told as children and the stories we tell ourselves about our divorce are part of what keep us settled. And some of those stories had their roots in things that happened to us long before we got married.

Because I was so young when my parents divorced, I have no conscious memory of them ever living together. My mother eventually remarried, but there were a few formative years when I had no model for what it was like to be parented by two adults in the same household, nor did I have a model for what it would be like to *be* one of those two parenting adults.

It took me years to realize it, but I formed a subconscious story from this early experience. And that story, as dumb as it sounds when I write it "out loud," was that once my husband and I became parents, he would, eventually, leave. It was, after all, what I had experienced as a child myself. Emotionally, if not intellectually, I carried the expectation that I would be a single parent. Unsurprisingly, I parented like one.

In my world, being a Good Mom meant taking on almost all the parenting duties by myself. I see now, though I didn't then, that I cut my son's dad out of the picture in small but insidious ways. I did all the co-sleeping, and was more or less fine with my ex sleeping in another room because he had insomnia. I did all the feeding (telling myself it was a pain to express breastmilk, which it was, but I seemed to have overlooked that it would have been nice to have given my ex the experience of nurturing his son). I made most of the parenting decisions, and I told myself that I was more competent (how?) to make them. Many years before we actually separated, let alone divorced, I relegated my son's father to the status of "Fun Weekend Dad."

My point isn't that you did or are doing these same things, or that you are the reason your marriage ended. My point is that who you are now as a single mom has its roots in not only your essential and socialized self (who you were born as and who you were taught to be), but also in the relationship your parents had with each other and how you were parented by them. It even goes back further than that, because your parents were the parents they were because of the way *they* were raised. If we go back far enough, we can find traces of your parenting style in some great-great-great grandparent you never even knew.

Ugh! Does this mean you are doomed to act out whatever marriage-and-parenting play your ancestors created in the distant past? No, absolutely not. It does mean that you have stories that inform who you are as a person and as a parent, and that without awareness of these stories and how they affect you, they will continue to run you. Left unchecked, they become the wagon wheel ruts we settle into, and they can stand in the way of your and your kids' happiness.

Let's sit with this for a moment. What do you know about the way your grandparents were raised? How about your parents? Can you see any connection between their experience and the one you had growing up?

As you think about this, pay extra attention to family sayings and beliefs, from generalized clichés like "Children should be seen and not heard" to family-specific stuff like "We're just unlucky, we always have been."

When I did this exercise recently with a small group of divorced moms, they were both entertained and startled by some of the weird things that came up. One woman told us that she had never done well in gym class, and she realized that it was because she had bought into her mom's story that the women in her family were all clumsy. She had actually preferred being labeled as unathletic to standing out from the rest of her clan.

Another mom had always felt guilty that she had never really been into snuggling with her kids when they were small. In thinking about it, she realized that in her family, wealth and success had been measured by her grandparents having made their way from a small walk-up in New York where six kids slept in a single bed to a suburban ranch where everyone had not only their own bed, but their own room. Snuggling wasn't seen as a value, it was seen as poverty and failure.

And me? I was in college before I realized that my favorite color wasn't blue, like my mom's, but green. But oh, how I had wanted to please her and be just like her! Because if I liked blue, just like her, that meant I was nothing like my dad. Who was, as previously mentioned, mentally ill. Given what I believed was a binary choice, I was very eager to be exactly-like-mom/not-crazy.

Our stories don't always begin with us. But we definitely hold the power to end them, amend them, or trade them in altogether. We'll be talking more about how to choose a better story going forward, and why it's pivotal to the art of *Un-Settling*.

Your Marriage Story

What kind of marriage did your parents have? Your grandparents? Most of us tend to unconsciously either recreate the marriages that were modeled for us, or, more consciously, strive mightily to achieve their opposite. Imago couple's therapy is based almost entirely on the theory that we marry our opposite gender parent in an attempt to work through whatever was left unresolved in childhood. I married a much saner and kinder version of my father. Interestingly, my ex married a version of *his* dad, albeit in female form, when he hooked up with me. We did actually work through our respective dad issues together. Our marriage, however, didn't survive the effort.

Looking back, can you find any similarity between your ex and either one of your parents? Were you looking to replicate a relationship from your childhood, or trying to resolve the unfinished business of one? Perhaps you found one or both of your parents so difficult that you ran as far and as fast as you could in the opposite direction, making sure you married someone as *unlike* your problem parent as humanly possible?

If this is hard to see for yourself—one of the reasons why my clients work with me is for an outsider's objectivity—look around at your friends or extended family. I bet you can easily discern that your favorite office buddy married a woman who belittles him just like his mother did, or that your bestie's ex was cold and withholding, just like her dad.

Be gentle with yourself here. Your marriage story might well have been part of why you eventually divorced. This doesn't make it *your fault*. This is actually how life is supposed to work. One of the better things we humans do, as we come together and sometimes pull apart, is help each other grow.

Your Parenting Story

Just as our past informs who we choose as our mates, so does it inform our parenting, causing us to model or react in counterpoint to how we ourselves were raised. My mom grew up under the semi-tyrannical thumb of an emotionally distant and irrationally punitive mother who, before any conflict could be resolved or closure could be reached, died when my mom was a young teenager. Mom told me that she may not have known much about how to parent, but she was clear on what *not* to do. Her siblings, my aunt and uncle, told me the same thing.

Can you see in your own relationship with your kids the ways in which you are recreating or reacting to the parenting you received as a child? This isn't a good/bad thing, unless you remain unconscious about it. My mom, for example, was intentionally respectful, kind, warm, and loving—precisely because her mother had been the exact opposite. My father, on the other hand, was both a creative and loving parent as well as an unconscious perpetuator of some of the very stuff he railed against in his own mother: overprotectiveness, neediness, and inflexibility.

I know you've had more than one occasion when you've opened your mouth and something your mom used to say to you popped out. It's disconcerting, isn't it? But it isn't necessarily a bad thing. It's important, however, to get conscious about our parenting story and how it impacts the way we're raising our kids. Power—and *Un-Settling*—begin with awareness.

Your Divorce Story

Whether you and your kids were in physical danger and it was imperative and obvious that you needed to get out or whether you and your ex just sort of drifted apart and there was no clear "that's it!" moment, there's what objectively happened and then there's the story you tell yourself (and others) about what happened. That's normal, and even necessary. We're storytellers by nature, we humans.

It's when those stories reflect an older, darker pain—the kind of unexamined yuck that keeps us stuck—that it's time to throw open the door and let a little light into the room. My story, for instance, that men leave once they become fathers, turned out to be a painful over-generalization and untrue. I was also completely blind to it until after my divorce. Had I not finally done the work to see it as the story it was, I would still be operating from it and treating guys like they might leave any moment. I might even be viewing my teenage son with suspicion; after all, isn't he going to grow up and "abandon" me, too?

The actual specifics of your marriage and what brought it to an end are unique to you. But it's interesting that the stories that we tell ourselves about what happened often have a surprising degree of commonality. It may be because our stories are often based not only on our own outdated information (what we observed from our parents' marriage, for example), but also on unreliable sources (gossip, social media), or even fiction (movies, books, TV). While some of us may be on a second or third marriage, others of us had never experienced divorce until, suddenly, we did. We reach into our pasts and look to our culture to help us make sense of what happened.

Whoa, Trigger!

When my clients tell me about their recent divorces and their lives since, they are often still triggered and speaking to me from a dark place. Darkness knows only one way to spin the story—predictably, that would be as grimly as possible. Worse, Darkness believes that the version of the story it knows is the gospel truth. It has to. Perpetuating painful stories is the only way for your Darkness to survive—and no matter how much pain dark energy causes us, it seeks to perpetuate itself by trying to trick us into buying its lies as fact. Your dark side would like you to settle. Pretty much forever. Because to the dark side, settling feels safe, and that feels infinitely preferable to risking anything, including happiness.

Neuro-linguistic Programming (NLP) talks about living *at cause* or *at effect*. Being at cause means that you take responsibility for what you want to create in life, and, further, take responsibility for the outcome of your actions. Your world is a place of infinite possibility, and you take intentional steps to move toward the life you want, the person you want to be. You believe that you have choice and control over your behavior and your results. You are *Un-Settling*.

At effect means blaming others or circumstances for failures, missed opportunities, or your unhappiness. You live in the land of "if only," sure that if something or someone else— your mother, your father, your boss, your ex, your kid—would just be different in some way, then everything would work out. In the meantime, you settle for whatever *less-than* you have been perpetuating.

When we are unaware of or feel helpless regarding our stories, we are forced to live at effect. We don't have a conscious understanding of why things happened, or what our role was in creating it, so we certainly don't feel we have any degree of control over what happens next. We feel powerless to earn our own happiness.

We definitely don't see that our stories are optional: narratives over which we have the ultimate say. But when we're able to make that shift—to pull a loose thread of even the most tightly woven fabrication—we step into light, and we stop settling. We realize that we are the storyteller, therefore we have control over our tale's outcome. How deliciously *Un-Settling*!

Victim or Victor Exercise

In a notebook or on your computer, I want you to write the story of your divorce and its aftermath, everything that led up to where you are now. Actually, I want you to write two versions, both of them using the actual facts and events as they unfolded. In the first, I want you to channel your inner Charles Dickens and make it as tragic and pitiful as possible. You are the hapless victim, Olivia Twist, so to speak, and you have been undone at the hands of evil-doers and horrid circumstances. Even if your divorce and your life since feel legitimately terrible without any embellishment, I want you to exaggerate here to cartoonish proportions. Don't change the facts. Don't change the circumstances. Just make it as awful as it can possibly sound.

When you're done, you are going to want to take a break. Even if you don't want to, I recommend that you do. Get up, shake it off, get some water, have a good cry, scream into a pillow, walk the dog. Do whatever you need to do to get yourself back to stable, if not neutral, space.

The next part is way more fun. On a separate sheet of paper, or in a new document in your computer, I want you to use the exact same facts and the exact same events, but this time, I want you to tell your story as a triumph. You are the heroine, emerging brave and victorious no matter what life and your ex threw your way. Your divorce and your actions since have been an epic journey, the stuff of legend, and if your story made it to the screen, someone insanely awesome like Beyonce or Linda (*Terminator 2*) Hamilton would play you.

Go on, take a victory lap around your living room. You earned it.

The point, in case you haven't figured it out, is to drive home that both of these versions are stories, and the slant you give them is independent of the actual facts, events, and circumstances. You get to choose which story you want to tell, in this as in everything else.

This is a cool exercise to do with kids of any age. Younger kids will like telling you or acting out a story with costumes, animals, or dolls. Older kids prefer writing it out, and may not want to share their efforts with you, which is perfectly okay. When everyone in the family understands that they can choose how to frame the things that happen seemingly "to" them, it's a massive leap forward toward collectively creating a happy new normal.

The Divorced Mom's Worst Fear

My client Maureen spent the first few weeks she worked with me settling for a story that may sound familiar to you: "I blew up my kid's life." The guilt and shame she felt over raising her child in a "broken home" (her words again) were profound, and the burden was heavy enough that she trudged through her days with a sort of grim determination.

Since Maureen did not yet perceive this as a story but instead saw it as fact, she behaved accordingly. She had destroyed her child's life and any chance at happiness, she believed, so it followed that she was a terrible person who deserved in some manner to be punished until such unidentified and unknown time when she would have sufficiently atoned.

And punish herself she did. She relived, over and over, the day she and her ex told their daughter, Jules, that they were getting a divorce. How Jules's face had crumpled, how ineffectual Maureen had felt, trying to hold and comfort her child even as Jules struggled to get away and run upstairs to her room. Every time Maureen started to feel like maybe things were going to be okay, or even—shhhh!—good, all it took was that single, searing memory popping seemingly unbidden into her head, and she would be right back to self-flagellation.

Are you thinking about the day you told your kid you and your ex were getting a divorce? It's potent, isn't it? It was a terrible, terrible day, one of the worst you may have ever experienced. Every divorced mom has been through it. Most of us eventually process it and come to see it as part of a larger, necessary, change we chose to bring about. We stopped settling and claimed a bigger, better life for ourselves and our kids. Maureen, however, was really looking for her proof that her story, "I blew up my kid's life," was true. Keeping this story in place was essential in order to continue to settle, and settling, while sucky, felt safe.

Ironically, Jules was more or less fine. Yes, it had been an awful day and a hard few months after, but Jules knew that her parents weren't getting along, and though she couldn't have articulated it at the time, it was as much a relief as a gut-punch when she learned they were splitting. At the point Maureen started working with me, Jules was alternatively trying to reassure her mom, with varying degrees of frustration, that she was okay, and playing her; an intelligent pre-teen, Jules had figured out that pushing Maureen's well-worn guilt button bought her extra screen time, trips to the mall to pick out "a treat," and even, on one day when Maureen was feeling especially conflicted, a kitten.

It's important to note that even if Jules had *not* been fine, even if she'd been struggling at school, depressed, and floundering, Maureen's guilt and shame would not have remotely helped. Jules needed her mom to be, well, her mom, not a perpetual penitent who couldn't allow even a moment's happiness in the door.

Maureen and I worked together for a couple of months, during which time she was able to see that she had a choice about what kind of story she told herself—and Jules—about what happened. From there, it was a very small leap to Maureen seeing that if she had control over the stories she told about her past, she likely had control over what she told herself about her present, and her future, too. She decided to stop settling for the disempowering version of her divorce story. She grew into the *Un-settling Mom* Jules needed her to be.

Thoughts vs. Facts

If you're like most of us, writing out your victim story made you feel some major yuck. When we tell ourselves and others disempowering stories, it's not exactly a big surprise that we feel disempowered as a result. The key question here is: Which story, victim or victor, felt more true to you? Which most resembles the story in your head, the story you tell others, and the story that forms what you think of as the historical record of your life? How much of it is factually true, as opposed to your opinion of what happened?

Now consider: whichever version of your story you chose as "most true," that's the story that drives your present-day choices, actions, and behaviors. It influences everything you do, from how you parent your kids to whether or not you believe yourself capable of creating and deserving happiness. Your story is what you model for your kids; it's the compass point you use to navigate your life.

Is your story taking you and your kids where you want to go? Are you living at cause or at effect? Do you see yourself as victim or victor? Settling or *Un-Settling*?

As many masters of "mental hygiene" have said before me, a thought isn't a fact, although it sure can seem like one when it's bouncing around in your head. In fact, the more painful the thought, the more insidiously it can masquerade as objective truth. And that's worth calling out, because if you've got painful thoughts that you are mistaking for fact, you're operating from bad information. It's like stopping someone on the street corner to ask them how to get to the train station, being given the wrong directions, and then blindly following them while hoping for the best. You're unlikely to get where you want to go. You can't get to Happy New Normal if your inner GPS is programmed, knowingly or unknowingly, with the information that will take you to Bummerville.

Many of my clients are confused by the difference between a thought and a fact. I mean, they know intellectually that a fact is observably and provably true, uncolored by opinion or slant, but in practice, that distinction becomes more murky.

Here's the example I usually give to help underscore the difference:

Fact: I have five dollars in my wallet.

Thought: I only have five dollars in my wallet.

See? All it took was the addition of one tiny word, and I've taken an objective fact—the amount of money in my wallet—and made it something I feel a little bad about. My circumstances, having a five-dollar bill in my wallet, remain unchanged. But the story I'm telling myself about it is disempowering and anxiety-provoking.

Yes, you worked through most of the grief over the end of your marriage, but you still have residual stories about it kicking around in your head. Equally important, you are telling new stories about your circumstances every single day, about your weight, your finances, your career, your kids, even about that guy who cut you off in traffic the other day. He was a total jerk, wasn't he? Entitled idiot. He didn't even look to see you. He just pulled out right in front of you, forcing you to swerve or brake, and kept going like he was king of the interstate.

Or, you know, he was a fellow human having a day. Maybe he'd had a fight with his kid or his partner. Maybe he was hurrying to get to work for a meeting he was going to be reprimanded for missing. Maybe his dog just died. Maybe he's a good guy but he just plain didn't see you.

We'll never know the objective truth of any of these stories, above. But what happens if you tell yourself the first story? You are angry; you are righteous. You surge ahead in traffic to try and look him in the eye, gesture angrily, or perhaps even try to cut *him* off. You seethe as you drive, so much so that you don't even think about the fact that your kids are in the backseat, watching, listening, and *learning*. When you get to where you're going, perhaps you'll cram an entire donut in your mouth in frustration, or take to social media to complain about terrible drivers.

If you tell yourself any of the alternative stories, however, you have compassion. You feel neutral, at worst. You go about your day. You live your life.

Every day, you model for your kids whether to live at cause or at effect. Whether to settle or *Un-Settle*.

Don't Believe Everything You Think

How do you know whether the thoughts you think and the stories you tell are true or not? The answer is so simple that many people struggle to accept it at first:

If your thought or story makes you feel terrible, it's a lie. Simple as that.

Has it ever occurred to you that you don't have to settle for the thoughts and stories that come up and fly around inside your head? I find this ongoing examination of my thoughts and the weird things my brain comes up with absolutely fascinating. You will, too, once you're willing to accept that your thought is just a data point, evidence of something going on for you that may or may not have anything to do with objective reality.

And, more importantly, that may not be serving you at all to continue to believe.

As an example, let's look at Maureen's thought, since you've already seen me working a little with that one, and I can supply Maureen's actual answers. Maureen's painful thought was, "I blew up my kid's life." And at the time we started working together, she fervently believed it to be true. As in, objectively true. As in, provably true. As in, any person on the entire planet would agree with the statement, "That sucky mom Maureen blew up her kid's life."

Ouch.

But that was just Maureen's settling self-talk, and settling, as we know, speaks the language of fear. Fear says stupid stuff like "I blew up my kid's life," and then it seals the deal for us by insisting that these inflammatory stories are somehow factually true. "I think it," says fear, "and so it's real."

Fear believes in monsters under the bed, too.

I asked Maureen about monsters under the bed, actually, because it turned out Jules had been afraid of them when she was younger. Although Maureen couldn't identify her own fear as fiction yet, she was able to see the parallel with her daughter. The monsters under the bed were legitimately frightening, but Jules' fear, no matter how real, didn't make the monsters real, too.

Then I asked Maureen how thinking this thought, "I blew up my kid's life," made her feel. Her answers tumbled out. She felt nauseated and anxious. She hated on herself just a little. She second-guessed whether she should have ended her marriage or whether she should have sucked it up and kept the family intact for Jules's sake.

It sounded awful, and it was. Maureen was so obsessed with the negative thought that she had ruined Jules's life that she was incapable of positive action. She felt guilty, so she let things slide at home. She did all the chores, in order to make things up to Jules; she bought off her guilt by buying Jules treats (remember the kitten?) She also overate, binge-watched Netflix, and nervously picked at the dry skin on the soles of her feet until, only once in a while, they bled.

I waved an imaginary magic wand in Maureen's general direction. "Let's pretend," I said, "that I magically whisked that thought away. You are no longer able to hold it in your head. How does that feel?"

Maureen's whole face lit up. "Free," she said. "Like I could just get on with it and focus on what's next."

Un-Settling: The Power of the Story

You are not a passive prisoner of your thoughts, and your thoughts may have only a tangential relationship to reality. Check this out for yourself. Start with a small thought, not the biggest one in your self-flagellating arsenal. See if your thought holds up under gentle challenge.

Remember The Three S Words, the ones that keep us stuck in settling? They were Shame, Second-guessing, and Stress. We talked about the common thoughts and fears that are behind The Three S Words. Let's look at them again, framed as painful thoughts:

- I made a mistake.
- I messed up my kid.
- I messed up the rest of my life.
- I won't thrive financially.
- I will die alone/never have another partner.
- I will find a partner, but will make all the same mistakes.
- I will never be truly happy again.

Yuck! Yuck, yuck, yuck. I'm sure it was obvious to you the first time around that these are painful thoughts to be carrying around, but now you can see why letting them gain a toehold directly impacts your results. No matter how much I want you to be happy, no matter how much you want to be happy, you cannot be happy with this kind of garbage taking up valuable energy and real estate in your brain.

And the above are just the most obvious painful thoughts many of us experience post-divorce. We humans have an estimated 50,000 to 70,000 thoughts *per day*. As you navigate this unknown single personhood and single parenthood in which you find yourself, what are the odds that you are only choosing the good ones?

Here's an interesting experiment: keep a small notebook or your cell phone with you, and note and/or record every painful thought that you notice. Obviously, you're only going to catch a fraction of them. But I think you'll be surprised, and maybe a little horrified, at how many self-defeating thoughts are flying through your head, often just below your level of full awareness. Most of us keep up a sort of running narrative, usually critical, of what we do and how we are showing up. In stream-of-consciousness form, it can sound like:

> *Ugh the alarm I shouldn't have stayed up so late got to get in the shower don't look in the mirror AUGH YOU LOOKED IN THE MIRROR I am so fat where did that weird line under my eye come from the towels smell a little funky I've gotta do laundry why can't I be more organized I can't seem to get it together oh no out of shampoo again so forgetful lately maybe it's early onset Alzheimer's I hope my kid remembered to set an alarm and is getting ready I should have woken her no that's enabling I have to be better at letting her learn on her own hate this razor why don't I have a better razor I need a pedicure they're expensive I'm not earning enough that jerk should be paying me alimony why didn't I ask for alimony I'm a pushover AUGH I LOOKED IN THE MIRROR I AM SO FAT....*

And you haven't even made it out of your bedroom yet.

But, wait a minute, I hear you saying. Wait! If I have 50,000 to 70,000 thoughts a day, I will never be able to keep track of them all. I'm thinking negative thoughts all the time and I'll never be aware of them and so I am doomed!

Let's get clear: a fleeting negative (or positive) thought isn't going to make much difference either way. It's the ones that persist, that come up over and over, the ones to which you consciously or unconsciously give your energy, that either tangle you up or free you. You don't have to worry about managing every single thought you ever have—it's not humanly possible, nor is it necessary. Instead, focus on the ones that feel heavy, the ones that are repeat offenders, the ones that stand out from the background noise.

Which brings me to another point. Don't beat yourself up about having painful thoughts. It will be tempting, once you see the sheer number and scope of them. But "I must stop thinking these painful thoughts" is a painful thought in and of itself. If beating yourself up isn't making you happy, trust that beating yourself up *harder* isn't going to make it better.

Instead of judgment, try curiosity: "Huh! That's a pretty terrible thought there, isn't it? Isn't it interesting that I've been thinking that thought?" Get curious about how it would feel to think a different thought. Try one on for size. Note your results, and decide if you want to settle for your original thought, try the new one, or go for yet a different thought altogether. Made a choice you don't like? No worries. Make a different one.

You are the woman who refused to settle for a dysfunctional, untenable marriage. You got yourself and your kids out. Why in the world would you now settle for horrible, self-limiting, painful stories that don't serve you and that keep you and your kid stuck and your life small? This is at the heart of *Un-Settling*: choose the stories you can leverage. Tell the stories that serve.

CHAPTER FOUR

Motherhood, Manifestation, and Money

*She'd had to make so many decisions. Whether to separate.
When to divorce. Where to live. What to say to other people.
What to tell little ears.
Now she found herself stuck on simple things: what movie to
watch, which boots to buy. Blue or gray? Hair up or down?
Chicken or fish?
So many choices; so little clarity.
She used to know exactly what she wanted. Where did that
clear-thinking, strong-minded woman go? And who was this
overwhelmed and dithery person in her place?
She peered at her screen and, with a click, transferred another
infusion of cash from savings to checking. She tried not to wince
at what remained.*

One of the most positive, most *Un-Settling* things you can do for you and your kids is learn how to attract better experiences and set your dial for happy. Overwhelm, lack of clarity or specificity, the inconsistent ability to make empowering choices—they all negatively impact your kids as well as you. Not to mention that waffling and overwhelm are probably not your top choices for what you want to model. It's tough to teach kids to make sound choices if you yourself are settling for stagnation and indecision.

Life after divorce can seem like walking into a new restaurant and being handed an elaborate menu. You hadn't expected to be dining alone, and yet here you are. There are a bunch of things that look like they'd be great. There's some stuff you've never heard of and aren't even sure how to pronounce. There are dishes you tried once long ago and didn't like, but wonder if you should give a second chance. And there is the tempting safety of the familiar, that old reliable grilled salmon, the chopped salad, the Pad Thai—it used to be a family joke, the way you'd always order the Pad Thai. Maybe you should just play it safe and order it again.

While it's exciting—you could ask for anything you want!—it's also overwhelming. If you're not going to settle for familiarity, what then? Ask what's popular? Order whatever the next table over is having? You could try telling the waiter to just bring you something good. But who knows what the waiter likes? You could end up with a plate of desiccated liver and onions. One thing's clear. If you keep just sitting there, not ordering anything, you're never going to have a chance at getting what you want. Is that the life you want for yourself? Is that what you want to model for your kids?

You and the Big U

Quantum physics tells us that everything—you, me, your kids, the Empire State Building, our thoughts—is made up of energy, vibrating at different frequencies. Some things vibrate so slowly they appear to be solid, like the desk at which I'm now sitting. If I knew how to match my vibration to the vibration of my desk, I could, theoretically, put my hand right through it.

From this standpoint, there is no energetic difference between our thoughts and our reality. This is why, in a 2014 study of basketball players at the University of Chicago, the group told to simply imagine making perfect free throws every day improved just as much as the group told to actually practice making perfect free throws every day. Our brains can't distinguish between real and imagined experience. Imaginary free throws fire the neural sequences and release the hormones and chemicals that create muscle memory, just as "real" free throws do.

Cool beans! We literally think ourselves into being. We are active creators of our own reality. "Whether you think you can or you think you can't," said automobile mogul Henry Ford, "you're right."

Do you think you can?

Maybe you read or saw *The Secret*, or you've heard something about the Law of Attraction. Both are based on the concept that we attract what we think about and give energy to. And it's not just woo woo, it's science; physicists tell us that like attracts like, and most of us, intuitively or experientially, know this to be true. Imagine someone moving through their day with the thought, "My life is overwhelming." Maybe that someone has even been you. What kind of actions, what kind of day, do you think the thought "My life is overwhelming" attracts? I'm betting chaos: unpaid parking meters and tickets, blown deadlines, snapping at service people and offspring, maybe even an emotional meltdown. There's no way to create goodness with the rallying cry, "My life is overwhelming." It's not a choice, it's not a cleanly expressed want, it's just a wail of frustration. Frustration, like anything else, tends to perpetuate itself.

It can sound too good to believe, this idea that we could change things just by changing our thoughts. We want to both resist and embrace it. Most of us are willing to believe that the thought "My life is overwhelming" is capable of actually creating more overwhelm. But we are almost afraid to believe that the thought "My life is amazing" could attract more amazing experiences.

Remember when I told you that Jess turned her and her daughter's life around with a single decision? You just learned what that decision was. Jess decided to stop settling for the garbage that was rattling around in her brain and to choose better thoughts. And once she did, she got different, better, and delightfully *Un-Settling* results.

Learning How to Decide

When you got divorced, you dared to stand up for yourself and hold a boundary around what you wanted and what you didn't. You were and are brave. *Un-Settling* is simply a continuation of what you already started. You can leverage that experience of standing up for yourself and your kids, and build on it.

I'm going to go out on a limb and posit that you actually *do* know what you want, and far more often than you think. But maybe it feels scary to admit it, or you've exhausted yourself making decisions, or you've broken trust with yourself (could it be that having decided to marry the guy you're now divorced from, you no longer have faith in your ability to make good choices?). You might be paralyzed by the fear that whatever you do next will negatively impact your kids.

It might help to know, right up front, that you're going to make some terrible decisions. It's part of the whole being-a-human deal. It's how we grow. Making the occasional terrible choice (aka invaluable and yet painful learning opportunity) is infinitely preferable to abdicating and making no choices at all. You might as well be back in that restaurant, everyone heartily enjoying their dinner all around you while you sit in indecision and hope the waiter will bring you some breadsticks.

The problem, for many of us, is that the very part of our brain we use to make choices shares cranium space with the part that will second-guess and argue with us about whether or not we're right. That part of your brain—some people call it the lizard brain, because its self-protective impulses come from the most primitive, reflexive part of us—would be happiest if Nothing Ever Changed, Ever. Change is scary. Change could put you at risk. Change could mean the difference between taking the same, safe path back to the cave and taking a new path that leads you right into the maw of the saber-toothed tiger.

If you imagine this part of your brain as being something close to a frightened toddler, you may be able to have more empathy for it. That toddler just wants to protect herself, and you. And good news: you know just how to deal with frightened toddlers. You listen, you acknowledge their fear, you assure them that you've got this, and then you distract them. Look, here's a pretty ball! Your toddler is part of you, and needs to feel heard. (Just try ignoring a toddler who really wants your attention!) So acknowledge, reassure, and move on. Don't hand her the keys to the bus.

Admitting to yourself what you want takes practice, so I recommend lots of it. If it feels less daunting, start with smallish stuff: put things into an online shopping basket (you don't have to actually buy them); choose a different route home from work; see what your body (not your brain) feels drawn to at the supermarket. Order something you've never tried at the restaurant.

There's an interesting study about decision-making and happiness. Two groups of art students were told to sketch five pictures in 60 minutes. Both groups were told that their work would be "turned in" for further study, but they could keep the one picture they liked best and take it home. One group, however, was told that they had to make the decision on the spot, because the pictures had to be "sent out" in the mail right away. The other group was told they could take their favorite picture home, but that the mail wouldn't go out until the next day, so they could come back and change their minds until then.

When they followed up months later, the members of the group who had to make a decision on the spot were very happy with the pictures they'd chosen. They all thought they'd gotten their very best one. The other group, however, wasn't happy at all. Almost all of them regretted their choice, and were sure that one of the other pictures had actually been better.

Fascinatingly, the group who had more time to decide felt they had *settled*. The group who had responded powerfully, quickly, and instinctively were confident in their choice.

Making strong, clear decisions without regret is a learnable skill. You'll want to get good at it, and you'll want to teach your kids how to do it, too. It is one of the cornerstones of *Un-Settling*.

Learning How to Ask for It

After you make some decisions and get clear on what you like and don't like, what you want and don't want, it's time to clearly ask for it.

Remember when I said that how you show up for your kids is how you show up for everything? Here's a perfect illustration. The way you ask (or don't ask) for what you want from your kids is the way you ask (or don't ask) for what you want from yourself, and from the world. It's also likely to reflect the way you were able (or unable) to ask for what you wanted during your marriage.

My client Susan articulated something I think a lot of women—including me—have felt: "If he had really loved me, he should have known what I wanted." This held true for her whether it came down to her ex getting her what she'd hoped for on her birthday, kissing her goodbye every time he left the house, or taking more of a leadership role with the kids. Her sense of grievance was real. We've all been there. But the fact was, Susan never actually told her ex she wanted any of these things; she expected him to intuit her desires as proof of their love and connection.

Unsurprisingly, after her divorce, Susan communicated with her kids in much the same dysfunctional way. She kept meticulous track of what her kids wanted and didn't want, liked and disliked, because she was outwardly, not inwardly, focused. She couldn't understand why they weren't equally tuned into her. Every time an opportunity arose for them to disappoint her, she was, inevitably, disappointed as expected, and then she sulked and withdrew. Sometimes she told herself that they just didn't care about her. When she told herself this story, she acted from it, pretending to care little about them, too.

You can cut this kind of settling off at the pass by asking simply and clearly for what you want, with no expectation and no emotional strings attached. For example: "Hey, I'm going to watch this movie I downloaded. I think you'd like it. Want to watch it with me?"

Accept that both yes and no are perfect answers.

Going Out for the Pass

If you want to catch the ball, you have to go out for the pass. Makes sense, right? But a common misperception of the Law of Attraction is that all you have to do is believe. As if you could rock back and forth on your bed and chant, "I have a million dollars, I have a million dollars," until somehow the money appears. But manifestation is more than mouthing mantras; it's about matching intention with inspired action. Expecting it to work without any effort on your part is like yelling a destination to your car's GPS from your bedroom and expecting you and your bed to somehow be magically directed and delivered there.

Your car's GPS is an excellent way to think about the Universe. Your GPS will take you anywhere you want to go, but it can't do it unless you get in the car, start the engine, and give it your intended destination. Imagine telling your GPS, "Just take me somewhere good," or "I don't know, just do whatever you think is best." How far do you think you'd get?

Like the Universe, your GPS has no judgment about your chosen destination. You want to drive to the worst neighborhood in town? Okey-doke. It'll tell you the most efficient way to get there. You want to drive to a spectacular view? It'll tell you how to get there, too. And if you make a wrong turn and end up someplace you didn't want to go, your GPS will simply course-correct (sometimes annoyingly, but still). It won't make you sit and review all your terrible choices and ask that you atone for all the wrong turns you took before it will direct you forward.

In other words, the Universe hears you and hears you literally, whether you ask for something negative or something positive. I learned this the hard way, long before I knew anything about manifestation or recognized that I was, in fact, manifesting.

You may remember my mentioning that I was bedridden, off and on, for years. Although I'd been a healthy kid, I started having headaches and digestive problems in high school. By the time I was a senior in college, I had TMJ, an ulcer, acid reflux, endometriosis, and transitive joint pain. Six years later, I was flat on my back with Chronic Fatigue Syndrome. 20 years after that, I'd be struck with biotoxin illness from exposure to mold.

How in the world could I have been asking for this? Well. I grew up watching my (divorced) parents, who both had separate and unrelated health issues, and I had concluded that there was power in illness. Sick people, six-year-old me observed, seemed to get whatever they wanted. They got out of doing things they didn't have to do. It felt to my little girl self that the world revolved around people when they were sick. They got all the attention. I wanted some of that for me, too.

When we accept a painful story like this, we are settling for exactly what we don't want. I didn't want to be sick. I just wanted to be seen and heard. I wanted to feel powerful. I wanted to matter. *Un-Settling* meant challenging this story, and my son was a huge impetus here. I had settled for decades of illness. I was determined that he not do the same.

One day, a friend of mine with similar health problems announced that she was moving her kids to a remote island where the environment was cleaner and where she hoped they would all recover their strength. I was impressed by her bravery, but it made me take a long, hard look at my choices, and whether I would ever do the same.

Nope, I decided. I was going to make a stand right here in Colorado with my kid. But I could do something differently radical. Instead of changing my environment, I could change my thoughts. Instead of "There is power in illness," I began practicing the thought, "I find my strength in good health." This was something I could get behind modeling for my kid.

Once I'd gotten used to thinking that thought, I found myself better able to act from it. I saw an acupuncturist, an Eastern medicine practitioner, a functional medicine doctor, and a chiropractor. They all helped me in different ways. As I began to improve, I started doing the things that the version of me who would become vibrantly healthy would do: I walked my dog in the foothills of the Rockies, even though at first I could only walk the equivalent of a block. I choreographed and danced a single show tune, alone in my living room, while I waited to be strong enough to go dancing in public. I filled my home with inexpensive furniture in vibrant colors that made me feel happy, and that reminded me of the more expensive versions to which I aspired. I threw potluck dinner parties, imagining the day when I'd cook the whole thing myself.

In other words, I "acted as if" I were already healthy. And in doing that, I became so. Today, I walk a mile or two a day (that may not sound like much, but for most of my adult life, I literally couldn't walk a block). I dance whenever I get the chance. I entertain, I travel, I go to parties. I weigh 20 pounds less than I did when I started writing this book, and I'll be at goal weight by the end of the year—because I got clear that the version of me who is a published author is not fat. In all these ways and more, I am calling in and acting from my future self.

The Secrets of Top Manifesting Mamas

One of my mentors, Michele Woodward, is one of the most powerful divorced moms I know. Her ex blindsided her by leaving her for another woman when their kids were 10 and 13. A former White House staffer, marketing executive, and lobbyist, she had taken a few years off from work to take care of the kids, so when her ex moved out, she was, as she says, "starting from scratch."

After she saw a free life coaching session offered at a charity auction, Michele began exploring the idea of becoming a coach herself. One serendipitous moment led to another, and within a year, she had trained with *O Magazine's* Martha Beck and was setting up shop. Her first August in business, she made $750. She remembers looking at that amount and immediately reframed it as the starting point from which she would take off and thrive. Today, she has a well-respected, financially and energetically successful, executive coaching and mentoring practice.

Michele made a point of checking in with her energy to make sure it was aligned with the outcome she wanted. She says, "Life is not a Disney movie, right? If you want a new life to appear, you have to line up behind that. Nobody's going to knock on your door with little bluebirds and give it to you. The only way to get there is to know yourself, love yourself, appreciate yourself, and line up behind that vision so that you are doing things every day to move yourself towards it. If you want a house with a pool, start where you can. Move into an apartment with a view of the pool."

This is at the heart of "acting as if." It doesn't mean spending money you don't have, living in blind denial of your present circumstances, or wandering about in a daze of delusion. It means creating a vision of the life you want for you and your kids, and then bringing as many elements of that future life into play in the present as possible. Manifestation expert Cassie

Parks, with whom I've worked and studied, recommends small actions like taking your kids for appetizers (my son loves tapas) at the fancy restaurant you see your future self frequenting every Friday, taking a route home from work that winds through the neighborhood where your future self lives with your kids, and creating travel itineraries for the trips your future self and your small band of merry-makers will be taking. Kids take to "acting as if" naturally and enthusiastically, by the way. Even teens, who are often trying on being world-weary for size, are still connected to a profound and powerful sense of play.

Michele has a daily morning and evening practice she swears by. "When I wake up, I might think, 'Here's what I want to have in my life today, here's what I want to remember, here's what I want to embody,' and then I'll get up and go to the bathroom," she says. "And then, at night when I go to bed, I lie there for a few minutes and think about what I'm grateful for. It doesn't have to be, 'I'm grateful I cured cancer.' It could be that I'm grateful that I built a fire in the fireplace. I'm grateful that I have the money to put gas in my car. The energy of being grateful for what you have is what brings opportunities to you."

Holistic health coach Jennifer Hooper admits she was in total denial when her husband raised the prospect of divorce; in fact, they lived under the same roof for the better part of the next year while she hoped to convince him to reconcile. But despite her initial resistance, she says now that "I'm very happy with the blank slate that I was given. I've been able to create a fresh start. I think that if I had stayed married, I would have been putting on a good show, but I wouldn't be nearly as happy as I am now. I have a lot more security, a stronger voice for myself, and the ability to define my own path."

Jennifer learned about manifestation principles from, ironically, a bad date. But after she'd done her own research, hired a coach, and started to see results, she started to see that date as the beginning of the rest of her life. She says that while she used to be an analyzer and a compromiser, she's since learned to get out of her own way, follow her gut, and make strong choices. Her results have been powerful.

"I drive a new car, I have a stylist, I live in my own home, last year I went on seven trips," she says. "I work 25% less, but I make three times more. Some of my girlfriends look at me with envy sometimes. I can do what I want. It's certainly not what I envisioned when I became married and a mother. But it's really good."

My friend Anella not only manifested an amazing life for herself and her kids post-divorce, she even manifested the man of her dreams (and wrote about it; you can find Anella's story in her book, *Hear Me Universe*).

"I believed initially that divorcing my husband would make my life so much better," Anella says, "and that everything that was unsatisfactory in my life was because of his presence in it."

She started dating, and after three years and three or four failed relationships, she had what she calls "this really clear moment when I thought, 'Oh, Anella, it can't be that every man in the world is flawed. It can't be that every one of them, including my ex, has a problem.' The recognition I gained was two-fold: first, that I was putting so much responsibility on a relationship or another person for my own happiness. And second, I asked myself the question, 'Well, then, what do you shift in you, kiddo?' And that question opened the floodgates."

Anella made a 100-item list of all the qualities she wanted in a mate, and within a matter of months, met her second husband and the man she considers her soul-mate, Craig. She believes that learning to let go of what was no longer hers to manage and leveraging the Law of Attraction to manifest the life of her dreams not only bettered her love life, but created an entirely new way of being for her kids, too.

"I think it was one of the greatest gifts of my divorce, for everybody," she says. "It allowed the kids to reach out and build something with their dad. It energetically opened up the possibility that they could all take independent action, and needed to take independent action, to develop relationships as independent people."

Anella is an *Un-Settling Woman*.

I recognize her, because I was raised by more than one of them: my mom, and my grandmother, Claire. Claire was perhaps one of the most *Un-Settling* women I have ever known. She was a force of nature, routinely doing things like flagging down a tour bus on Chicago's Lake Shore Drive and demanding the driver take her and my sister, who was suffering a mild asthma attack at the time, to her Streeterville condo while he was just sitting there waiting for his tour to come out of the Adler Planetarium. He did. In her later years, after she'd been diagnosed with cancer, she fainted in a drugstore. She'd come to by the time the ambulance showed up and was mostly irritated. She was fine, she told the paramedics, but she was late for her weekly hair appointment. She talked them into dropping her off at the salon after promising them she'd stop by the emergency room the moment her hair was done. (They did, and she did.)

There's a cool coda to this. Claire died on her own terms (the day she went to the hospital for the last time, she left her will and all her paperwork carefully laid out on her dining room table) at age 90. Even several years later, it's almost impossible to imagine that she's not out there somewhere, blowing red lipstick kisses and laughing her inimitable guffaw. But she wasn't done with us yet. The day before I wrote this chapter, my mom posted a picture of her new RV on Facebook. Surprise! Claire's condo had belatedly sold, after a long enough period of time that my mom and most of the rest of the family didn't even realize it was still on the market, and Claire had bequeathed enough money from the proceeds for my mom to pay off some debt she'd incurred during a difficult year of health problems and enough left over to buy that RV. At age 80, my mom is ready to hit the road and take on a whole set of new adventures.

My mom says it's an answer to her prayers. But with no disrespect to God or any other deity, I know it's from Claire. *Un-Settling* women take care of their kids.

How to Make Amazing Choices

Depending on the decision-making dynamic of your marriage, you may still be getting used to making solo judgment calls. I used to call my ex fairly regularly after we separated; I had grown accustomed to having him to bounce things off of, and it took me a while to adjust to doing it differently.

Jennifer ended up doing a lot of compromising and settling in her marriage. "With my husband, it was always, 'Someday,' or 'We can't do this,' or 'Why would you want to do *that*?'" she says. It took time for her to figure out her rhythm on her own. "I've learned that if I'm thinking really hard about something," she says, "it's not the right thing. I can go to the left. Or the right. Or go back and forth all day long. But if I go with the gut, then it's full speed ahead. And there's no back and forth. It's just forward."

How do you know what your gut has to say? There are many wonderful methods to learn how to feel into your body for answers, from muscle testing to simply developing and holding awareness of how "yes" and "no" physically feel to you. Making the choice from your body is a powerful practice. Your brain is perfectly willing to lie to you. Your body cannot. It's convenient, too, since you take your body with you everywhere you go. We'll be talking more about this in the next chapter.

"Acting as if" is more than just behaving as if you already have what you want. It's also bringing yourself into alignment with your future self and what she feels, thinks about, and gives her attention to. I mentioned, for example, that my future self isn't fat. As soon as I realized this, I was able to lose weight. For the first time in my life, I was led by my decision to eat differently—as opposed to waiting to lose weight before claiming the life a thin, healthy person would lead.

What choice would your future self make, the *Un-Settling Woman* who already has the life you want? My future self, for example, doesn't worry about debt—because she has none. And in order to make sure my present self also doesn't worry about it, I put the one credit card I have on autopay from my bank. I don't have to think about it or give it any of my energy, because it all gets taken care of behind the scenes. Similarly, my son buys a mysterious amount of food from the school cafeteria, especially considering I send him with a sack lunch. My future self doesn't worry about stuff like this, so I have his account with the school on auto-pay, too.

When we make decisions from the perspective of our future selves, we are tapping into the magic of the Universe and our own inner wisdom. I'm going to guess that your Future Self is no longer worried about whether or not her kids are okay. What would that look like? How would a mom who wasn't worried about her kids behave and talk? What actions would she choose? Would she settle for the experience you're giving yourself? Or would she *Un-Settle*, and step into a more powerful way of being?

When I was at my most worried about my son, I used to pounce on him after school and grill him the moment he got into the car: "How was your day? Did you have fun? Was anyone mean to you? Are you feeling okay?"

Ugh, right?

It took concerted effort, but I forced myself to stop with the interrogation methods and simply give him space to be. When he wasn't being forced to deal with my fear and negative expectations, he was calmer, and the odds that he actually had a good day improved. He also opened up, talking to me much more readily than he ever had before.

What's the More *Un-Settling* Story?

When I am presented with an A/B choice for which there appears to be no single, obvious winner, I like asking myself a simple but surprisingly powerful question: What would make the better story?

That may sound flippant, but sit with it a moment. Which story would you want to be telling, one year, five years from now, sitting among trusted soul friends? Still not sure? Think about your absolute best stories. The ones that make you feel something when you tell them. The ones that make others tear up, or crack up. Which story seems like one of those? Which will you be happy one day to repeat?

Some examples from my most *Un-Settling* stories: what led me to rent a car and drive from Chicago to Ann Arbor to argue my way into the University of Michigan; the time I put on my best "Step away from the door!" voice and defended a fellow journalist from what was literally an angry mob; and how I ended up soaked to the bone, stark naked, and jumping up and down on the handles of my open apartment window in full view of several gawkers in the apartment building across the way.

Nobody's best story goes anything like: "There was this thing I thought I maybe wanted to do, and I almost did it, but then I didn't." This isn't to say that everything you choose has to be epic, which sounds sort of exhausting. But framing your choice as a future story throws an interesting wild card into the mix that is surprisingly clarifying. You could tell a story about a perfectly enjoyable evening spent slobbing around the house and binge-watching Netflix. Once. The next day. But you're not going to get much mileage or pleasure out of telling it over and over, years hence. And you're probably not going to love telling the story of how you chose this experience, over and over, night after night.

Choose the better story.

Show Me the Money

No matter how much money you make, the fact remains that where you once had a two-income household, now you have one. Your divorce likely cost you; even my own DIY divorce, in which neither of us sought child support or alimony and there was no dispute over assets or debt, was surprisingly expensive in filing fees alone.

Money doesn't measure your inner worth, but it is, like it or not, the means of currency we've all agreed upon. Cash can't make us happy in and of itself, but what we do with it, what experiences and feelings we enjoy because of it, are an integral part of a fully abundant life.

There is no reason to feel ashamed of or weird about wanting more money. And there is no reason for you to *settle* for anything less than abundance.

Our unresolved money stories can get in the way of creating that amazing life we want to model for our kids. A longstanding money story, for me, was one my ex and I originated: "We always have just enough." We were sort of proud of this—it seemed thrifty and non-greedy—but it made us perpetually anxious, since we zeroed out at the end of each month. We were never truly in need. We were also never truly prosperous.

The Universe fully cooperated with our story that we always had just enough. If an extra $3000 came into our lives, we could be sure that the furnace would break, or we'd need a ridiculously expensive car repair. It worked the other way, too. If an unexpected expense came up, we could be sure that we would find the money. But only barely.

This felt good. But it was also limiting and exhausting. We never got ahead. We never had more than we absolutely needed right that red-hot second. We were often white-knuckling it toward the end of the month. And as for savings? Out of the question.

This wasn't going to fly after my divorce. My household had lost one income, and my dreams of where I wanted to take my life next required funding. So my first order of business as a divorced mom was to change my story. It just needed a small tweak: "I always have more than enough." I began to act, in small ways, as if this were true. I took my son out to dinner (happy hour and appetizers) three or four times a month. I invested in my business. I gave to charitable organizations. I kept a $20 bill tucked into a small compartment in my wallet so that I could say, with total honesty, "I always have money."

And, almost immediately, things began to change. I decided to go on a hunt for spare change and found a crazy amount of money hiding in my couch cushions, my car, even the drawers in my kitchen (why in the world had I put cash there?). I landed a surprise writing gig just in time to splurge a little more than usual at Christmas. I signed up with a program to manifest $10,000 in 90 days, and manifested $20,000 by replacing one long-term (difficult) client with a new one that was much more in alignment with my passions and my purpose.

I believed in this stuff already, but even I was blown away.

My client Gillian had dug a big enough hole for herself after her divorce that she was just plain afraid to believe in money manifestation. In order to continue her kids' piano lessons, substantial allowances, and high-end soccer camps, she had maxed out her two major credit cards and was considering applying for a third. Instead, I invited her to take a look at her thoughts. We started with her money story. Gillian's parents had raised her to believe that having money was sort of shameful and embarrassing, and that people who were well-off were either gaming the system or over-privileged jerks.

But when I asked Gillian to tell me about at least three people she knew who were financially abundant and whose ethics she admired, she had no problem coming up with examples, both from her personal life and in the media. Armed with a new story, that money was a tool she could use to create not only abundance for herself and her kids but also make a positive difference in the world, Gillian started to get some wiggle room and small amounts—a refund from an accidental double-payment here, a coupon there—started to show up for her.

Gillian joined a credit union, worked with a debt counselor, consolidated her credit cards, and set up automatic withdrawal payment plans. She talked to her kids, who were far more aware of her financial stress than she had realized, and they were willing to cut their allowances in half, temporarily, while the family re-set its financial goals. She also created a vision board rich with representations of the experiences abundance would enable her to enjoy, and affirmed for herself on a daily basis that she and her kids deserved financial success.

Most importantly, she began looking for ways in which abundance was already appearing in her life: her expense account at work allowed her to enjoy restaurants she might not otherwise have felt she could afford. Her parents loved hanging with the kids, so she saved money on child care. Her loving circle of friends had helped decorate her new, post-divorce home with their own donated, free artwork.

In less than a year, Gillian cut her debt in half, got rid of one of the credit cards, and, with the money she saved on interest payments, took her kids to a dude ranch over summer break. Instead of perpetuating her family's story that money is the root of some unnamed evil, Gillian chose to *Un-Settle* and change the plot. Her kids have their own bank accounts and are learning how to maximize interest and rewards points. Money is no longer the great unmentionable; in fact, she and the kids like to talk about their respective investments and what they're saving up for on Friday pizza nights.

Don't let your own skepticism—or that of anyone else—get in your way.

One day, not too long ago, I had an unexpected expense come up. As I drove my son to school, I told him, "I'm going to manifest a couple thousand dollars today."

He, ever the teen, rolled his eyes and said, "Yeah, right."

I said, "No, I want you in this with me. Pretend that you think this is going to happen."

He sighed. "Okay, fine, I'll pretend you're going to manifest a couple thousand dollars today."

After I dropped him off at school, I checked the mailbox. There was a check for $97, a reimbursement for something I had completely forgotten about. "Oh, cool," I thought, but I stayed open to finding something more.

By the time my son came home from school, I had over $3500 that had fallen into my lap, none of it expected. I met him at the door and told him right away.

He one-eyed me with a bit of a grin. "I guess I'm gonna pretend this stuff works," he said.

Manifesting abundance doesn't always look like a five dollar bill on the sidewalk or a check in the mail. In fact, sometimes it looks like a crisis. My client Barb took her son's wonky cell phone to the store and was told she'd have to replace it to the tune of over $1000. She was willing to do so, but her gut whispered to her to do her due diligence. So she went home, got a customer service rep on the phone, and learned there was a known bug in the Google software preloaded onto her son's cell. By following her instincts—and changing one setting on the phone—she saved herself a cool grand.

Manifestation, like most things, gets easier with practice. You can start by simply building your awareness. Pam Grout, in her best-selling *E-Squared*, suggests picking an unusual car color (I picked lime green) and then just counting how many of them you see over the course of the day. (I found a staggering 42 in an hour.) Want to raise your game? Ask to be shown feathers, or heart-shaped rocks; you'll start seeing them in the most unexpected places. Ask your kids to help you find them!

Work your way up from there: pennies, parking places, the best table in the restaurant. Whatever you set your sights on, I recommend adding, "this or something better." Don't get attached to how whatever it is will manifest, or even when. Mike

"*Notes from the Universe*" Dooley calls these "the cursed hows," and maintains that they are the Universe's business, not yours.

As I have become a more practiced manifestor, one of my favorite questions has become, "What else is possible?" It's a reminder to me that the possibilities are, if not limitless, then certainly vast, and that if I get out of the Universe's way, I leave space to receive more, and differently, than my sometimes-limited human brain could ever have dreamed of.

Sometimes, entertainingly, things manifest in a way that appears to be backward. As I am writing this chapter, I manifested a beautiful new home that virtually fell into my lap. (By which I mean I saw it on Craigslist, fell in love, and was the first person to see it.) This made no sense to me, because I have been happy in my tinier, more modest townhouse and there's only another year and a half to go before my son graduates from school. Why in the world would I move with only a year left?

I got my answer when I emailed my current landlord, checking to see what she might be raising the rent to next year. I think I was looking to be saved from having to step up into this bigger, more prosperous, more beautiful townhouse. She emailed me back telling me—much to my surprise—that she wasn't going to renew my lease for another year and that she wanted to move back in herself.

Suddenly, my manifesting that other townhouse made perfect sense.

Ooh, and it has my dream kitchen for cooking and entertaining—and a music room for my guitarist son. We moved in just before I started the final rewrite of this book. My life is amazing!

Don't Settle for Settling

Our culture promises that when we get *this*, then we'll feel *that*. When we lose weight, then we'll feel beautiful. When we get that new car, then we'll feel successful. When our kids are happy, then we'll be happy.

But like attracts like, remember? We can't attract beauty, prosperity, and happiness while feeling fugly, poor, and in despair. We must change our feeling state first, before anything in our external world can change for the better.

When I ask clients to identify the internal feelings they want for themselves, they often respond with externals instead. They'll tell me they want to send their kids to tennis camp, or pay off their attorney fees from the divorce, or get a better job closer to their son's school. None of those goals, as great as they may be, are feelings. So we do some digging to find out what's underneath.

"How would getting what you want feel?" I ask them. They are wary; for some reason this seems like a trick question. "Good?" they respond with an upward inflection; they want to get this answer right. But together, we get there, with patience and persistence and sometimes a square or two of dark chocolate. "I'd feel calmer," they say. "I'd feel confident."

Now these are feeling states we can work with. What, I ask them, are two or three simple actions they can take that would make them feel calm and confident *right now*? As long as they are waiting for the feelings to come first, those goals, that stuff, will continue to elude them.

CHAPTER FIVE

Practical Magic and Radical Self-Care

As she drank her morning coffee, she looked over her list. Actually, it was one of several lists she had going; she liked making lists because it felt she was doing something.

At the top of today's list: find a yoga studio. She hoped that if she could engage the kids in fun outdoor activities—biking to the Farmer's Market, hiking trails with the dog (once they got a dog, another item on the list)—maybe they would open up and talk. She rewrote "YOGA" in all caps, underlined it several times, and punctuated it with three exclamation marks.

This wasn't the first time yoga had been on the list, but today, she'd actually make the calls and do the Internet research. Probably. If she wasn't too tired.

She looked at all the other items on the list and sighed. Writing this all out felt great. Looking at it felt terrible.

Have you heard the oxygen mask metaphor so often it makes you want to puke? Get a barf bag ready, because here it comes again. As a life coach who has both told and heard this analogy more times than I can count, I still believe that it bears repetition, because even if you're nodding your head, you are most likely not really taking it in or acting on it. Far too many of us have been trained to think it's selfish to self-care.

So here we go, one more time. You and your kid are on a plane. The aircraft may or may not be going down, but the turbulence is insane. You're terrified, but you don't want to show it. Your kid is terrified, and you wish with every fiber of your being that this wasn't happening. But it is.

There's a weird shrieking sound from one of the engines and the oxygen masks pop out of the ceiling. You fumble with your kid's mask; their survival depends on you. But just as you're shakily trying to get it into place, wooziness from lack of air overtakes you. You pass out. You can't help your kid, because you couldn't bring yourself to help yourself.

In this hideous and over-worked metaphor, everybody dies.

Breathe. *This is just a story*.

But what happens if you get your oxygen mask on first, just like the flight attendant told you to do? You have space to breathe. You can think clearly. You can help your child, and maybe even several others around you. As long as the plane doesn't crash (and for our purposes, it's not going to), everyone will be fine.

Un-Settling means that you refuse to settle for anything less than the life you want to live. And that includes the self-care you need and deserve. After all, you're busy modeling an amazing life for your kids. Don't you want to model self-care, too?

Take Care of Yourself like It's Your Job

You don't *have* to take care of yourself, of course. For many years, I sort of didn't. My off-and-on health problems abruptly turned back on with a vengeance when my son was about nine. I'd let myself get so sick and burned out that I was literally bedridden.

You know what kind of mom I was from a completely horizontal position, unable to sit up or stand? I'm going to say "tangential." I read books to my son, we played games as best I could on my bed, we talked, he fell asleep with his head on my pillow. He was well-loved. But I had to rely on others to get him fed, dressed, bathed, to and from school, to soccer practice, to watch the soccer games and cheer him on, to take him to the dentist and the doctor, etc.

You are likely not ever going to deal with anything that extreme, but even so, when you are exhausted, depressed, immune-compromised from stress, out of shape, spiritually drained, or at the end of your emotional rope, there's no way you can show up like you want to for your kids.

And your kids are watching. It would be great if they'd do as we say, not as we do, but humans learn by imitation. There is a picture of my son, age two, taken when I was having one of my horizontal episodes. In it, he is curled in a fetal position on our couch, gazing blankly into space. He wasn't upset at the time.

He was imitating me. The photo is chilling, but I keep it to remind me that I am modeling for my son. But only *all the time*.

If you don't have physical, spiritual, and emotional support practices in place, it's paramount to your kids' happiness—and yours—that you start. It doesn't matter much what you do as long as you consistently do it. That might look like morning meditation followed by yoga and journaling. It might look like a good, sweaty run around the neighborhood while you breathlessly vent to your running partners and blow off steam. It might look like mani-pedis, massages, and spa cuisine prepared by your own personal chef. It might look like a support group at the church and a new membership at the gym.

My client Alana finds her peace in the mountains near her home, and in particular, on one spectacular drive up the canyon. She tells me the towering peaks are like the spires of a cathedral to her; she calls the mountains "my church." This particular drive is about 15 minutes from her home, but when I asked her how often she made it, she said only once every couple of months. I asked Alana to schedule this restorative drive on her calendar no less than once a week, and now it's a firmly embedded and much-cherished part of her Sunday routine. Bonus: once or twice a month, she brings the kids, who are learning to love it, too.

Find routines that work like this for you. Find someone to talk to, write to, vent to, or pray to. Move your body in a way that feels good to you, or at least in a way that you're willing to sustain over time. Find something to believe in, something bigger than yourself. Take in as many as or fewer calories than you expend. Make your bedroom sacred space; use it only for sleep and sex (have some—you are likely your own best partner!). Look for opportunities to laugh, and laugh hard, even if it's only at a cat video.

It doesn't matter which path you follow to make sure your oxygen mask is in place. Take care of yourself. It's your job; no one else is going to do it for you. And if you don't do it, you are simply not emotionally, spiritually, and/or physically available to take care of your kids.

Fill Your Days with Things You Love

I can almost hear the eye roll from here. I know. Your day already feels pretty packed with stuff you are indifferent to at best, and loathe at worst. How in the world are you supposed to add in anything else, let alone things you love?

One of the things I realized after my divorce is that I wasn't exactly sure what I liked to do. And my preferences seemed irrelevant anyway; I *had* to get things done, so why would it matter if I enjoyed them or not?

Let's just gently set aside the issue of whether or not you have to do everything you think you do, and focus for a moment on your feelings about it. Yes, even if they seem irrelevant to the task(s) at hand.

In the last chapter, I told you about the idea of tuning into your body for cues about your true feelings. Leveraging how you feel is easiest when you establish a baseline and learn how your body, in particular, expresses a heartfelt YES and a resounding NO. Some of us feel the former as expansiveness, or lightness, or excited tingles in our fingertips. Some of us feel the latter as nausea, or muscle tension, or—and I may be an outlier here—as an ache in the sole of the left foot.

In 2009, I trained to be a life coach with the divine Martha Beck. You may know her from her columns in *O Magazine*, or from one of her brilliantly funny and insightful books, like *Steering by Starlight, Expecting Adam,* or *Leaving the Saints.* In her first "coach-y" book, *Finding Your Own North Star*, Martha took the reader (and we fledging coaches, back in the day), through an exercise she calls The Body Compass.

Here's how it works. Simply sit with something you know was a bad experience for you. For many of us, it's the day we or our ex asked for a divorce, or the day we told our kids. But if these are too recent and too trigger-y, go for something a little further back in your past. Just make sure that whatever you're remembering is something clearly and obviously painful for you. Put yourself back into that memory as completely as possible, by recalling the time of year, the time of day, who else was around, how old you were, whether there are smells or sights or sounds associated with the memory. Can you taste anything related to this time?

When you feel like you're fully in the memory, scan your body from your toes to the top of your head, looking for anything that stands out. Numbness, tightness, aches, and heaviness are all common. Note that we are looking for *body sensations*, not emotions, though those will likely come up, too.

This constellation of sensations represents how your body feels when you are in NO space. Remember it, and think of it as -10 on a scale ranging from there to +10. The ranking is important, because we're going to use it in a little bit here to take you through a typical day.

After you've had a chance to shake off the energy of this experience (and please accept my apologies for putting you through it), do the same thing again, only this time with a memory of one of the best times in your life. Put yourself back into the experience, engaging as many of your senses as possible. Scan your body from your toes to top of your head, noting the sensations that come up, like lightness, tingling, feeling like you're flying or floating, a sense of expansion, and so on. This set of sensations is how your body expresses a full-throated YES. On our scale, this is your +10, the best you can possibly feel.

And voilá! We've now turned your body into a walking, talking barometer you can use to measure the truth of how you feel about anything and everything in your life, from putting a new roll of toilet paper on the holder (mysteriously, I hate this task with a passion) and Zumba to grocery shopping and playing Monopoly with the kids.

Next, get a sheet of paper and list all the tasks and activities that make up a typical day for you, from the moment you wake up until the moment you go to bed. Resist the urge to put your head down and cry. We are about to improve your life a hundredfold.

As you feel into each task *with your body* using the method described above, rate it on your scale of -10 to +10. Most things will probably fall between -5 and +5. Ignore those for now. Instead, make note of the things that fall at -5 or below or +5 and above.

You already know what I'm going to say, don't you? Do less of the things you hate; do more of the things you love. As long as we can find you the time, I doubt you'll need much encouragement to do more of the things that make you happy. So how are we going to find that time? Easy-peasy. We're going to get rid of some of that stuff you hate.

The Three Bs

This is a great follow-up tool, also from Martha Beck, and it's one of my very favorites to use with clients because it's *fun*. Once you master it, you'll be amazed at how much control you actually do have in your life. (Hint: this is a wonderful tool to teach your kids, too.)

The Three Bs are Bag It, Barter It, or Better It. Bag It means exactly what it sounds like: instead of continuing to do something you absolutely hate to do, you simply drop it from your list and accept the consequences. Barter It means finding someone else to do it for you, either by swapping tasks, by giving this task to someone who will do it simply out of the goodness of their heart (or because you're their mother and you will make them), or by paying someone to do it for you. Better It means that you are dealing with an unavoidable task that you and only you can do, but you will find some way to make it suck less.

Let's go to my client Christina for an example. Christina had two elementary school-aged kids who both had after-school activities twice a week. Christina's son Caden had soccer from 3:30 to 4:30. Her daughter Joley had advanced gymnastics from 5 to 7 pm. There was no time to go home between activities, and so Christina and Joley sat in the car while Caden played soccer, then Christina and Caden sat in the car while Joley worked out on the parallel bars. There was a lot of sitting in the car. Everybody found these evenings exhausting and stressful, and the various systems Christina had tried to put in place weren't working.

Christina checked in with her body, as I taught her, to tease apart each independent piece of this puzzle. She found she didn't mind being a chauffeur; she actually liked the chance to have one-on-one time with each child. She didn't even mind the long hours of sitting in the car; she read, and the kids got their homework done. But what she hated was trying to figure out how to get both kids fed (they would melt down if she waited until they got home at 8 pm). Christina was convinced the kids "needed a proper meal" that she didn't have time to prepare and pack up in advance in between rushing home from work, changing, and picking up the kids—and she was on a tight budget, so carry-out wasn't a regular option.

I took Christina through the 3 Bs. She obviously didn't want to Bag It and not feed her kids. She felt she couldn't afford to Barter It by buying ready-to-eat foods from groceries or restaurants. We agreed that her best option was to Better It—but how?

Christina found her answer when she took this problem to her kids, who had the best idea of all: Picnic Nights. Together, they found a basket that would work, and together, she and the kids started the night before to put together simple but fun foods that traveled well: fruit, sandwiches, crackers, cheese, raw veggies, canned soups and stews heated and packed in thermoses, occasional treats. Of course this was easily something Christina could have done by herself, but she Bettered It by putting her kids in charge of deciding what went into the picnic basket and giving them joint ownership over the task.

My client Beth, a painter and divorced mom with limited free time, wasn't painting. She told me she just couldn't summon up the energy after working at a graphic design firm all day. When I walked her through the individual tasks that made up getting ready to paint, she was surprised to identify that she had no problem with any of it—except the precious time she had to put in clearing away her son's photography equipment from the spare bedroom they both shared as a hobby room. This scored a whopping -7 on Beth's scale. It also made her hate on her life, just a little. She was settling for 9 to 5 when what she really wanted was to make and model the life of a fine artist for her son.

All it took to get Beth painting again was eliminating this chore (Bagging It) by setting her son's photography gear up in the basement in a space previously dedicated to an unused Bowflex. Her son was happy because he hadn't been loving sharing space with mom anyway.

Take a look at all those -5s and below on your list. What can you Bag, Barter, or Better? Don't settle for a bunch of energy-draining, time-sucking tasks in your life. Be willing to be *Un-Settling*.

CHAPTER SIX

Building Better Relationships

The kids were asking why their dad didn't call as much anymore. She didn't know for sure. Maybe he was depressed. Maybe he found it easier to disconnect than to feel the sadness of parenting via Skype. Maybe he was just being a jerk.

Every time they left to be with him, she felt both the giddy freedom and the empty ache of being alone. Her nest was half-empty; her glass felt half-full.

She missed the family banter around the table, but she was also grateful not to have to endure the angry, highly charged silences that had characterized the final months of their marriage.

Now, she and the kids all seemed to eat at different times. She'd read that this was bad for kids. Of course, she'd also read that divorce was bad for kids. That ship had obviously sailed. How was she going to create that sense of family now?

Giving Up

Many wise minds have written about the freedom of letting go, but I like the blunt comfort of author Anne Lamott the best: "Forgiveness is giving up all hope of having had a better past."

In other words, there's the pain of what happened, which is considerable. But it can pale against the agony of believing that whatever happened *shouldn't* have happened. There is no way to reach back into the past and make it turn out differently.

This is a hard truth for us to grab onto. But listen to the impossible, irresolvable conflict here: It "shouldn't" have happened; but it did. He "shouldn't" have done it; but he did. You "should" have done something differently; but you didn't.

That way lies madness—or, at the very least, many very long nights lying awake with the bile rising in your throat as you replay what you did, what he did, what happened next, and argue with it. When you fight with your past, you fight with reality, and you fight with yourself. This is a no-win proposition, and it keeps you angry, off-balance, and in the energy of recrimination. In recrimination, you are constantly struggling for the moral high ground. And it can be its most insidious when that struggle is with your past self.

My client Hannah was tormented by the fear that she'd left her marriage prematurely, despite the fact that her ex had told her that he loved her but was no longer "in love" with her and had moved to the guest bedroom down the hall, where he spent hours setting up online dating profiles and chatting with strangers. Although at the time she was clear that she didn't want to settle for a sham of a marriage, she had since had read articles and blog posts by women who advocated hanging in there and fighting for your family, and she wondered, now, why she hadn't. "I should have tried harder," she told me. "Why did I just roll over?"

Some of us torment ourselves by replaying the worst moments of our marriage; some of us gloss over the painful parts and remember things as having been better than they really were. Hannah was among the latter. In order to support her painful belief that she "shouldn't have left so easily," she was subconsciously but willfully forgetting the many nights her ex didn't come home; the worried questions from the kids at the breakfast table; the way she covered for him out of both maternal concern and crushing humiliation. It took three sessions with me before she even mentioned the blood tests and terror she'd had to undergo after he told her he might have been exposed to HIV.

When Hannah and I talked about her ex, she offered me considerable insight into and context for his actions. He'd had a difficult childhood, she told me. He found it hard to deeply connect to others, and was more comfortable with superficial interaction. He had been passed over for a promotion at work, and he'd felt powerless and small.

Significantly, she had no such compassion for herself. She tormented herself with what-ifs. What if she'd insisted more strongly that he get help? (He'd refused, saying that she was the one with the problems, that he was perfectly happy.) What if she'd waited him out? (Surely it was a phase, albeit one that had gone on, at the time of their separation, for almost two years.) What if she'd taken a lover and reconciled herself to having a roommate instead of a spouse? Maybe that would have been better for the kids.

What-ifs are totally irrelevant and counter-productive, but at first, Hannah wasn't willing to concede that. So we walked down the path of each of her scenarios to what were, inevitably, untenable hypothetical outcomes. But even if any of those scenarios could have resulted in a potential happier ending, they were still the stuff of magical thinking. All of her what-ifs came down to the same thing: what if the past had been different than it actually was?

The answer may sound harsh, but take it in, because with truth comes a key step toward *Un-Settling* freedom. Yes, if things had been different, then things might have come out differently. But it's senseless to give this any of our energy, because things *weren't* different, they were exactly as they were. Once Hannah was able to breathe into this and accept it, that things had gone the way they had gone and that all the what-ifs in the world weren't going to change it, she was able to set herself free of her past. She was able to be present and to be at peace with herself and her kids.

Second-guessing is almost second nature for many divorced moms, and understandably so. We believe that we chose wrongly at some point, either by marrying the guy in the first place, or for not seeing what was happening, or for not getting out sooner, or for not staying longer and trying to make it work. We worry that our choices, his choices, have hurt our children. It can be really hard for some of us to come back from that.

But come back to ourselves we must. Because when we are in disharmony with ourselves, we are out of alignment with our souls, our world, and our kids. Forgiveness begins at home, and the person we must start with is us.

The Art of Self-Forgiveness

Your kid comes to you with a confession. They broke something important to you. They knew when they were handling it that it was fragile, but they messed up. They dropped it. It's in shards, and it's not fixable. They are in tears and terrified of your response.

Are you mad? Maybe. Are you disappointed? Almost certainly. Do you wish that they hadn't touched it, that it had never happened, that this thing that was so important to you was somehow still whole? Of course you do.

So you take their hand, and you look into their tear-stained face, and you say:

"OH MY GOD, what is WRONG with you!? You are a TERRIBLE PERSON! You have HURT ME TO THE CORE! There is no way to fix this and nothing will EVER BE THE SAME AGAIN! Now go to your room and think about what you've done FOR THE REST OF YOUR LIFE!"

What, does that sound ridiculous to you? If you're a sane person, I'm guessing yes. But is it all that different from the internal dialogue you have with yourself, like, every night after the kids have gone to sleep?

Your marriage is broken. It's over. It's not fixable. Either you broke it, or he broke it, or the two of you broke it, or circumstances broke it and you guys couldn't overcome them. Whatever the case, it's done and in shards. Are you going to keep picking up the pieces and poking yourself with them until you bleed? Or are you going to clean them up, dispose of them properly, and move on with your life?

Let's go back to your child who broke that thing you loved. In your mind, ask your child these questions and "hear" their response:

What did you do?

I broke something important to Mom.

What are you making it mean?

That I'm bad. That I deserve to be punished. That the punishment will be awful.

What would compassion say?

I didn't mean to break it. It was so beautiful, I just wanted to touch it.

What did you learn?

To look with my eyes instead of my hands.

What do we say?

I'm sorry, Mom.

What happens next? Well, unless you are one stone-cold mama, you probably give your child a hug. *You forgive them.*

What, that's it? Yes, that's it. Consider what you did (or think you did, which is tantamount to the same thing—if you believe it's so, you are operating from the feeling that it's so). Ask yourself what you are making your action or inaction mean. Consider a more compassionate viewpoint—ask yourself what a loving friend would tell you, until you can do this for yourself. Learn from it; there is always something to be taken forward from any regret. And now, consider it done. *Forgive yourself, and let it go.*

Un-Settling: Creating a New Us

It is almost every divorced mom's first instinct to keep everything as much the same as possible for her kids, and nowhere is this more evident than in our relationship with them. We tell our kids as much when we break the news of the split: "Mommy and Daddy aren't getting along anymore, but we still both love you, and that will never, ever change."

The deep abiding nature of our love for them does not, of course, change. But our relationships must. No matter how abusive, absent, or amazing your ex was and/or is, he's no longer living with you in your home. You and your kids are on your own now. And no matter what the circumstances, you can choose to make this a positive thing.

One of the shards I chose to pick up and stab myself with after my ex and I separated was that I had voluntarily "given up half my son's childhood" via joint custody. I had wanted shared custody and I supported my son having a strong and positive relationship with his dad, but I hadn't done the math, and I hadn't reckoned on how many hours, days, weeks, and even years that meant that I wouldn't be under the same roof with my kid. I was devastated once I worked it out.

But that was all about quantity. What I hadn't taken into account was that the quality of our relationship would change, and for the better. We both became more honest and transparent with each other. We found our own inside jokes and rhythms. We discovered shared activities we might not have if I'd stayed married to his dad. I might have fewer hours with him than I did before (and this is arguable, because even when two parents are under the same roof, the whole family doesn't do everything joined at the hip), but we get *more* out of those hours than we ever did before.

I've always loved my son. What I discovered in the years after the divorce was how much I *liked* him, too. We have a relationship that is utterly different than the one we would have had if I'd stayed married to his dad. Not better, not worse, but different, and really good. I am absolutely confident that the bond we've created will hold.

This didn't happen overnight, or even over the course of weeks and months of nights. Developing a new sense of "us" is a process, one that you grow into and that evolves over time. Sometimes, that path is even a rocky one, but that doesn't mean the destination isn't worth it. I'm so grateful I didn't settle for the sad little story about giving up half my son's childhood.

Audrey's emotionally abusive ex was determined to undermine her relationship with her boys. He told them that she was the one who'd cheated, that she was the reason their marriage was over, and that she would continue to lie and hurt them every day they stayed with her. None of this, by the way, was factually true.

She was devastated, but chose to, as she says, "come back to what I call the ground zero of love. No matter what they're feeling, don't try to argue them out of it. Hear them, and give them an authentic, sincere, loving interaction. Stop worrying, stop talking at them, stop trying to manipulate their experience."

One of her sons, Liam, bought her ex's lies and chose to go live with his dad. The other, Jake, stayed with her. Determined to *Un-Settle* and forge a better relationship with him, Audrey stopped talking and started doing. She cooked dinner with Jake. She took him hiking, camping, and kayaking. When he expressed interest in learning to hunt, she made sure they both knew how to shoot and handle weaponry safely, got her license, and took him pheasant hunting, which she says was "horrific." She didn't roll over and give in to whatever Jake wanted, but as much as possible, she tried to meet him where he was and take an interest in the things he wanted to do.

The next time her ex lied to Jake, she asked Jake to consider his experience of her and whether she had done or said anything that would indicate that what Jake's dad had told him was true. Jake was able to look back at months of positive experiences and see that his dad's stories didn't hang together or make sense.

Audrey, who is both an artist and a professor of philosophy, puts it beautifully: "People often think that when you're drawing or painting, you draw this beautiful thing right out of the gate. But I know as an artist that you have to do 25 drawings that suck, that are painfully not fun to draw. And then that 26th drawing is beautiful and looks effortless," she says. "I know that if I hadn't pushed with Jake, that if we hadn't done swimming and camping and cooking together even when it was hard to afford and I was exhausted, we couldn't have been where we are now."

You Are the Alpha

You are an *Un-Settling Mom*. You are the alpha of your new family and your home.

One of the biggest lessons I learned was to stop checking in with and deferring to my son so much of the time. Because I felt I had "done" something big to him that he hadn't asked for (the divorce and, subsequently, a cross-country move), I was consequently so eager to "make it up" to him that I was trying to give him control over every other aspect of his life. It was well-intentioned, but misguided. Instead of giving him the reassurance of clear structure and strong parenting, I was behaving like his subordinate and making things weird. I'd ask, almost conciliatorily, that he do his chores around the house. I'd ask if he "wanted" to go to the store with me and help me carry bags. I'd ask him to spend time with me. I'd ask him, over and over and over, if he was okay.

It took me a pathetically long period of time to figure out that whatever I asked, whenever I asked, his reflexive answer was almost always non-committal, a brush-off, or a flat-out no. I was acting like a diffident and apologetic B & B host when what my son absolutely needed was for me to alpha the situation and be his mom. I'm not advocating being a martinet and imposing draconian measures, but it's important for you and your kids that you establish your house rules, maintain boundaries, work out the consequences of your kids making questionable choices (even better if those consequences come naturally, like taking a lower grade if they don't do their homework), and create new routines they can count on.

This doesn't need to be humorless and grim, and it shouldn't be all work and no play. My son and I still enjoy Game Nights, even though instead of playing Monopoly and Minecraft (thank God!), we're now playing each other our favorite music on YouTube and laughing until we cry over Cards Against Humanity. We also make it a point to go out to dinner together at least once or twice a month. We have some of our best conversations in restaurants (and he's willing to try a wider variety of food than he is at home).

Your kids are looking to you to decide whether things are or ever will be okay, just as they did when they were tiny. Back in the day, whenever my son had a small mishap, I used to turn up my hands, give an exaggerated shrug, and say, cheerfully, "Uh-oh!" His first words were literally "Uh-oh," sung out happily after dropping a Cheerio off his highchair tray.

This doesn't mean negating your child's experience. If they're hurting, grinning manically and shouting "Uh-oh" at them is just plain mean. But if you get still and pay attention, you can discern the difference between your kid being in trouble and your kid testing the waters. You can affirm that the water is safe, the temperature is fine, and that, together, you will make it to the other side.

Un-Settling Moms raise *Un-Settling Kids.*

The Man Formerly Known as Your Husband

Unless your ex put you and your kids in harm's way (and if he did, I hope you are miles away from him and that he doesn't know your whereabouts), it's probably safe to assume that you'd like to have as easy a co-parenting relationship with him as possible. I say "as possible," because in some instances, like Audrey's, communications break down to the point where a no-contact policy is the only thing that makes sense. Only you can know if that's the case between you and your ex.

The rest of us have a wide range of normal when it comes to our relationships with our exes. After a few initial months when it just hurt us both too badly to talk much, my son's dad is now very much a part of our lives. He lives a couple miles away; we talk on the phone several times a week, and we have been celebrating our son's birthdays and Christmases together since the split. But we, I have come to realize, are not the norm. Most of my clients and divorced mom friends have a more complicated relationship with their ex-husbands. Some of them have no relationship at all.

My mom never spoke ill of my dad, though she had good reason to. But she didn't like being alone in the same room with him (he would wait outside in his car until I got home from school when it was his turn to pick me up), and he used to write his child support checks out to me, refusing to use her new last name once she remarried. I was strongly aware of both these things, and I suppose it may have influenced how I chose to interact with my son's father post-divorce.

But I couldn't have done it alone. No matter how cordial I may have wanted things to be, if my ex had not been a kind and open-hearted man who wanted the same thing, we would not be where we are. And if that had been the case, that would have to have been okay, too. Letting go of how things (and your ex) "should" be is the fast track to reclaiming your *Un-Settling* self.

Ellen, who has since remarried, has had the opportunity to see this play out to both extremes. She realized not long after she married that her first husband wasn't "that into her" and, further, that he wasn't "that into" the concept of work. But she stayed for the kids until it became clear that she was alone in her life, with or without him. She chose without.

Her ex has since been consistently angry, vengeful, and willfully negative. Attempts at family gatherings devolved into him shouting at her and upsetting their now-adult children to the point that they will no longer tolerate having both of them visit at the same time. Her oldest daughter recently called her, crying, "Mom, I can't believe you allowed this to happen with Dad. I can't believe you guys can't come together on some level to make this okay. I can't go to any family things anymore."

Ellen hates this situation, but she knows it's not her. That's because in her second marriage, she's had an entirely different experience with her husband and *his* ex, Martha. Martha didn't like Ellen at all at first, but Ellen, refusing to repeat the same experience she'd had with her own ex, insisted that the whole family, including Ellen's stepson Benjamin, all go into counseling together. Now, Martha and Ellen get along so well that she says they're like family. "It's so gratifying," she says, "to see how happy Benjamin is. All he's ever known is 'Team Benjamin.'"

Remember in Chapter 5, when we talked about asking for what you want? Here's what's under your control: get clear on what you want, and make sure you clearly ask for it. Hold true to your vision of what a good relationship with your ex would look like, and hold up your end of the bargain. But know that asking for what you want is no guarantee that you'll get it. Sometimes the answer is yes. Sometimes the answer is no. Sometimes the answer is not yet. If things aren't where you want them to be, it could be that you just need to give it some time. Even my ex and I went through that period of almost a year when it was just gut-wrenchingly hard to talk, and so we mostly didn't.

And it could be that things will never be exactly as you want. And that can be okay, if you let it. No matter how good or how bad your relationship with your ex, these are some of the things that help:

- **Release blame**. It doesn't matter now who did what. It's over.
- **Forgive yourself**. And, while you're at it, forgive him. You were both doing the best you could with whatever level of self-evolution and awareness you had at the time, which may have been very little. You don't have to condone anything. Just breathe and see if you can let even a little of it go.
- **Set firm but loving boundaries**. It hurt my ex terribly when, in the last months of our marriage, I made a rule that if my bedroom door was shut, he could not come in and talk to me. But I was sick and needed rest, and there were times when I simply couldn't handle another emotional conversation. Similarly, it hurt me when, after we split, he would sometimes back out of phone calls, telling me, "I'm sorry, I thought I could talk about this right now, but I was wrong." Get clear on what you can handle and what you can't. Speak up before you get

to the point where you're no longer in control of your feelings. If you don't want your ex dropping by without calling, or coming into your home without knocking, say so.

- **Make it about the kids—but only when it's actually about the kids.** Even acrimonious exes can often hold it together for parent-teacher conferences, joint decisions, shared concerns, and attending extracurricular events. That said, it can be tempting to start conversations "about the kids" that then veer off into old, wounded territory. Watch out for sandbagging (sneak attacks like "He's just like you, he's so *disorganized and irresponsible!*"), piling on ("You missed after-school pick-up, just like you missed *every important occasion of our lives* for 15 years!"), and bait-and-switch ("Hey, I called to see if you'd mind switching weekends because I've got a thing this Friday, but I know you and *that guy you've been sleeping with* planned to go skiing, are you sure you should be exposing the kids to that so soon?").

- **Pick your battles.** What's more important: that your ex return the kids at the exact top of the hour, or that he loves them and they had a good time? Keep your eyes on the prize: no matter what your relationship with your ex, you want your kids to have a good, healthy relationship with their dad. Hold onto this when you're tempted to go off on him.

If you aren't happy with the relationship you have with yourself, your kids, your ex, or the world, change has to start somewhere. Stop settling for things you don't want. Since you have little to no control over the actions, choices, and feelings of others, *Un-Settling*, it's clear, must begin with you.

CHAPTER SEVEN

How You Get in Your Own Way

It felt like for every step forward, she and the kids took one or two steps back.

When one kid finally stopped acting out, the other started.

She lost ten pounds, then twisted her ankle and regained twelve.

She finally went on another date—and the guy interrupted her even more than her ex ever had.

In the meantime, her ex was suddenly acting all happy, *and she didn't know why. Things were still patently not okay; what in the world did he have to be happy about? The kids said he had promised to take them to Paris. How could he do that when he knew that had been* her *dream and also that there was no way she could afford it now?*

She Googled nearby hotels with the vague idea of booking a long weekend's "staycation" so the kids could enjoy the pool. It was

obviously inferior to Paris, but she needed to stay competitive here.
Didn't she?

Change is hard, even positive change. Your lizard brain is threatened by it (don't get eaten by the saber-toothed tigers!), and your brain resists it. Here's why: every thought you have, every action you take, forms a new neural connection. The more you repeat that thought or action, the stronger that connection becomes. The thoughts and behaviors you've repeated many, many times have neural connections that are as strong and entrenched as mighty oaks. But the new ones, in contrast, are tiny, delicate little tendrils, just beginning to push their way up through the soil. Without frequent tending (which means thinking or acting on them over and over), it's easy for them to wither and die.

System Tug and Change-Back Attacks

In the 1950s, psychiatrist Dr. Murray Bowen posited that families, whether biological, cultural, or even business-related, are a system in which every member is affected by the actions of any other, sort of like a group of mountain climbers lashed together. If one gives up, falls, or tries to break away from the team, the other members experience "system tug," a literal or figurative tug on that rope that they are unlikely to find pleasant or reassuring. The natural response is to resist. The system demands that everything change back to the way it was.

This is one of the biggest obstacles to true, meaningful, and lasting change: not everybody in your life actually *wants* this for you, though they may believe that they do. Change (*Un-Settling*) is threatening to the system, just like it was at the Academy we called school. Therefore it's threatening for each member of it, too.

You may have experienced this in action already. Some common examples of system tug include losing weight only to have your favorite binge buddies tell you that you look too thin; showing up early at the office and having fellow staffers claim that you're making them "look bad;" even deciding you want to celebrate Christmas at home with your kids and your parents howling that you don't love them anymore. System tug is also the reason why, if a dysfunctional member of the system cleans up his act, another member will often step in to take his place—like when a black sheep cousin stops drinking and then someone else in the family starts dabbling with drugs. If you have more than one child, you've likely seen system tug in your own home on more than one occasion.

Change-back attacks are similar. In this dynamic, someone close to you is threatened by a change you've made in yourself, and wants you to STOP IT RIGHT NOW. My client Stephanie had been the peacekeeper of her large, extended family, but after going through a hard divorce and doing a lot of soul-searching, she realized she was exhausted from expending so much energy making sure everyone else in the world was okay at the expense of her own well-being. That Thanksgiving, she intentionally chose to stay quiet instead of jumping in to fill every silence or smoothing over every bump in the dinner table conversation. Later, as she and her sisters were doing the dishes, she found that everyone was angry at her. "What's *happened* to you?" one sister demanded. "You just sat there, *judging* everyone."

Since Stephanie had been feeling calm and neutral, she was caught off-guard by her sister's attack. She didn't know that her sisters were completely threatened by the change in the family dynamic and were thrown by the loss of the reliable and selfless version of Stephanie, the one who always stepped up and made sure things flowed for everyone else. Understandably but unreasonably, they wanted her to change back.

It's hard enough to make changes when everyone is rooting for you; it's incredibly challenging to do so when some of the people you love the most are subconsciously undermining you. Your kids, by the way, are likely to be at the very top of the list of those who will resist change. You may think you're strong enough to fight off the criticisms of petty co-workers and sniping sisters. Will you be able to hold strong in the face of your children's pleas, anger, and quivering lower lips?

My clients tell me that one of the best things about working with a coach is that they have an accountability partner, someone who will hold space for them to step into the change they want to embody, and who will notice and gently challenge them when they fall back into old habits and ways of thinking. You may find that a good and trusted friend can do this for you, but careful: even your most loving friends may not want you to change as much as they think they do.

Your Ex May Become More Awesome Without You

Even when we feel generous enough to want our ex to be happy, it can still feel weird if he gets to his "happy new normal" before we do. But remember: divorce is transformational, for him as well as for you. It's not unusual for exes to stop drinking, lose weight, have breakthroughs in therapy, discover a passion for salsa dancing you would have given your eyeteeth to share, or—worst of all—fall in love with someone else and treat her miles better than they ever treated you.

This is painful, but don't lose sight of the fact that you're not the only one watching. Your kids are paying close attention, too. This is your chance to walk your talk, the one you've been telling them about how the divorce was no one's fault, but sometimes parents just don't want to live together anymore and that's okay. Because it *is* okay. Truly. At least, it will be.

My client Lucy went through a particularly amicable divorce and spent the next few years celebrating holidays and feeling like friends with her ex. Then he met Melanie, and, in rapid succession, got Melanie pregnant, married her, and then, two years later, got her pregnant again—with twins. This turn of events immediately plunged Lucy into darkness. She brooded jealously about her ex's newfound happiness and worried constantly that she would lose her kids' affections to someone she perceived as a new rival.

"We were doing so well until she came into the picture," Lucy wailed.

Lucy picked at this open wound, comparing her lifestyle to her ex's and feeling that she was coming up short. "He lives in a bigger house, he's got all the bells and whistles, and now there are half-sisters to play with," she told me. "I'm beginning to get worried that the only reason the kids spend time with me is that they feel sorry for me, and they're trying to appease me."

The truth was, Lucy's kids were as freaked out as Lucy was by the addition of four new competitors for their dad's attention. But Lucy was so busy worrying about losing them that she didn't notice they were worried about losing their dad to his "new family."

It's hard to watch someone you once loved and who you feel let you down move on, especially if he learns from the experience and as a result does a better job with someone else. You want to be big and open-hearted; you feel small and bitter and petty. Lucy benefitted from getting an outside, objective perspective from a coach, someone who could call her out when her careening emotions got the better of her and nudge her gently back to herself. You, too, may need some help staying in your own lane.

And Now, Appearing in the Role of Your Dad …

Remember Anella talking about how she finally realized that every man couldn't be equally flawed, and that the answer lay within? If you find yourself reenacting the dysfunctions of your marriage with the guys you are now or eventually will start dating, it's because it makes all kinds of emotional sense. As we talked about in Chapter 4, you are likely re-creating the first relationship with a man you ever experienced: your relationship with your dad.

There is comfort and therefore perceived safety in the familiar, even when the familiar is highly dysfunctional. So be on the alert for this as you move forward with your social and romantic life. If you haven't resolved what went wrong between you and your ex (or you and your mom, or you and your dad), you are likely to keep repeating it.

Before you can avoid falling down that hole in the sidewalk yet again (Portia Nelson's oft-quoted and brilliant poem, *Autobiography in Five Chapters*, plays with this metaphor powerfully and beautifully), you have to be aware that it's there. Do your work on this, and enlist the help of an objective, outside viewpoint when you need it.

All Things in Divine Order

There is no magic timeline. There is no right or wrong. There is no one, single way to learn to *Un-Settle*. Coming back to yourself—to that fierce warrior mom who knew she would do anything to make a better life for herself and her kids—is a path with stepping stones shaped to fit your feet, and your feet alone. The way forward may not always feel obvious to you, but your willingness to move forward, to take that first step, is what will make the rest of the path appear. Walk on, *Un-Settling Woman*. Ask for someone to hold the flashlight when you need it. The rest of your life—and of your kids' lives—is waiting for you.

CONCLUSION

When she woke up that morning, something was different.
At first, she couldn't tell what it was.
She had slept through the night and she finally felt well-rested, but that wasn't it.
She could tell from the faint smell of pancakes that the kids had made their own breakfast, which was a small miracle. But that wasn't it, either.
She rolled over onto the other side of the bed, the one she usually avoided, and smiled as a shaft of sunlight caught her eye. There was a pretty view of the trees from here; why had she been sticking to the gloomier side of the mattress?
She stuck a foot outside the duvet and experimentally wiggled it around, testing the temperature of the air. There was a delicious breeze, scented with freshly cut grass and a hint of maple syrup. She heard music coming from the family room and the sound of her children's laughter. It was Saturday, and it would be for the whole day.
Anticipation. That was it. For the first time in a long time, she was actually looking forward to getting out of bed.

She started to reach for her laptop, then changed her mind. Her
children were waiting. So, she hoped, were the pancakes.

I never thought I'd get divorced. I'm guessing neither did you. And yet, here we are, you and me, standing in new territory, contemplating fresh vistas and wondering in which direction our happiness, and that of our children, lies.

You now have a better understanding of yourself, that complex amalgam of you as you came out of the box and everything you've experienced to date. You understand your strengths and challenges as a parent, as a person. You know that the choice of whether to settle or *Un-Settle* is yours, and yours alone.

You've probably uncovered more than a few yucky stories and painful thoughts you've been carrying around—some of them for many years. They're heavy, aren't they? You may not yet be ready to put them down, but you can imagine how it might feel if and when you do. It might be work, but invigorating work, like cleaning out a closet, like losing 20 pounds.

Like ending your marriage and letting go of all that pain.

You're still worried about your kids. Let's face it, you're always going to be worried about your kids. But there's "I hope he doesn't ding up the car" worry and then there's "I hope he won't end up hard and bitter and in years of therapy" worry. You're ready for some nice, normal, regular mom worry right now. It would be a relief, wouldn't it?

You've got a glimpse of some tools. How to get clear on what you want. How to use your body to help you make the best decisions for yourself. How to harness the power of your own thoughts to bring about the reality and the life you want to create for you and your kids. How to build better relationships with yourself, your young ones, your ex—heck, maybe even with some great new guy, someday, when you're ready.

And most importantly, you've come to readiness. Ready to stop settling. Ready to figure out what's next. Ready to take control of your life, make empowered decisions, and go all in, without second-guessing, without regret, without fear. You're ready to show yourself, the world, and your kids what *Un-Settling* looks like. You're ready to turn a corner, and to never look back.

I've worked with so many brave and brilliant women who've come to this point, this place where pain no longer serves, where stress is simply another way of settling and staying stuck. It thrills me every time I watch a single mom get a breath, step into her power, take her kids by the hand, and roar.

I believe you can take flight. I believe it, because I've done it, and because I've watched so many other women like you do it, too.

I hope you step to the edge. I hope you test your wings. The rest of the life you're going to create for you and your kids is right there, waiting for you. I can't wait to see you soar.

"There is freedom waiting for you,
On the breezes of the sky,
And you ask 'What if I fall?'
Oh but my darling,
What if you fly?"
– Erin Hanson

ACKNOWLEDGEMENTS

This book could never have been written without the ongoing kindness, compassion, and skillful co-parenting of my beloved friend and ex-husband, Tone McReynolds. Tone, one of my greatest joys is knowing you remain such an integral part of my life. Thank you for your generosity of spirit.

A humble bow to my master teacher, my son Desmond McReynolds. Back when I was having trouble conceiving, I saw a psychic who assured me that there was one energy, definitely male, hovering around me. "You and he have been around the block many times," she said, "but he's never seen you this angry before and he's not sure he wants to take it on." Thanks, Mr. B, for taking me on and choosing me to be your mom. Because of you and for you, I'm joyfully and irrevocably *Un-Settling*.

To my partner, Sky Kier: a big piece of my puzzle clicked into place when I met you, and I have been blessed to have you energetically at and on my side ever since. Thanks for the serious growth work, the playful silliness, and all the sighs and swoons.

My three dear parents gave their all to me, even and most especially when I didn't make it easy. To my mother, Nancy Brown, my late father, Chip Magnus, and my stepfather, Gary Brown: thank you for the unconditional love and for the deep-seated belief that I can do anything I set my mind to. You guys shaped me. I think I turned out pretty good.

Extended family: I am grateful to you and for you. Thanks to my sister Janet, my stepmother Phyllis, my late grandmothers Claire Crews and Margaret Magnus, and the rest of the Crews, Magnus, Conway, and McReynolds clans.

To intentional family, dear friends, and the many brave and wise women I've been privileged to work with: Dianne, Becci, Stacey, Peggy, Sally, Karen, Kris, Ellen, Marcy, Ruth, Lisa, Grace, RoseAnne, Diane, Cassie, and anyone I may have overlooked, you all are part of the tapestry. I see you.

To the Morgan James Publishing team: Special thanks to David Hancock, CEO & Founder, for believing in me and my message. To my Author Relations Manager, Margo Toulouse, thanks for making the process seamless and easy. Many more thanks to everyone else, but especially Jim Howard, Bethany Marshall, and Nickcole Watkins.

Finally, to my Author Incubator tribe, including Cynthia Kane, who asks the best questions ever, and the incomparable Angela Lauria, an *Un-Settling Woman* who dreams so brightly she can't help but shine light on all of us around her. All the hugs.

ABOUT THE AUTHOR

 Maggie McReynolds is an award-winning writer, certified life coach, divorced mom, and unapologetically *Un-Settling Woman*. She has studied with *O Magazine* columnist, author, and "America's Life Coach" Dr. Martha Beck, Mike *"Notes from the Universe"* Dooley, energy expert Dian Daniel, and manifestation coach Cassie Parks, and is a certified Infinite Possibilities Trainer and Trailblazer as well as a Raised Vibration facilitator.

Since Maggie's own divorce in 2012, she has been working to empower women and their children through small group workshops, and online programs. Although *Un-Settling* is not her first book (she was "published" in her school's library at age 10), it is the first to be seen outside the walls of Bottenfield Elementary.

Maggie lives near Boulder, Colorado with her son, Desmond, an unreasonable number of guitars, and a small dog who suffers under the delusion that he is a cat.

Maggie can be reached at maggie@maggiemcreynolds.com.

THANK YOU

If you're like me, this isn't the first time you've researched and read about divorce and how to mitigate its effect on your kids. I'm glad to offer concrete, actionable steps that make a genuine and lasting difference, and grateful to you for reading through to the end.

Just a reminder: go take **The Un-Settling Truth** quiz on my website to learn where and how you are settling and staying smaller than you and your kids deserve to be. You'll also find a free webinar outlining your best first steps toward *Un-Settling*, as well as an offer of a free strategy session with me to brainstorm what *Un-Settling* looks like for you, and how to set you and your kids on a path to an amazing shared life together.

Namaste,

Maggie

Website: iamunsettling.com
Facebook: facebook.com/themaggiemcreynolds
Email: maggie@maggiemcreynolds.com

Morgan James
Speakers Group

We connect Morgan James published
authors with live and online events
and audiences who will benefit
from their expertise.

Printed in the USA
CPSIA information can be obtained
at www.ICGtesting.com
JSHW082355140824
68134JS00020B/2085

9 781683 507413